antonio carluccio's ITALIAN FEAST

antonio
carlu

CCIO'S
ITALIAN
FEAST

WITH FOOD PHOTOGRAPHS BY
GRAHAM KIRK

BBC BOOKS

This book is published to accompany the television series entitled *Antonio Carluccio's Italian Feast* which was first broadcast in 1996. The series was produced by Bazal Productions for BBC Television.
Executive Producer: Peter Bazalgette
Producer/Director: David Pritchard

Published by BBC Books,
an imprint of BBC Worldwide Publishing.
BBC Worldwide Limited, Woodlands, 80 Wood Lane, London W12 0TT.

First published 1996
Reprinted 1996 (three times)
© Antonio Carluccio, 1996
The moral rights of the author have been asserted
ISBN 0 563 37169 2

Designed by Harry Green
Food photography by Graham Kirk.
All other photographs by Cassie Farrell, except page 5, by Priscilla Carluccio.
Props by Helen Payne

Set in Baskerville and Futura by Ace Filmsetting Ltd, Frome
Printed and bound in Great Britain by Butler & Tanner Ltd, Frome & London
Colour separations by Radstock Reproductions Ltd, Midsomer Norton
Jacket printed by Lawrence Allen Ltd, Weston-super-Mare

Any of the speciality ingredients used in this book should be available from good Italian delicatessens. A wide range is stocked at

Carluccio's
28a Neal Street
London WC2H 9PS
Tel: 0171-240 1487
Fax: 0171-497 1361

Details of other stockists of Carluccio's products may also be obtained from this address.

Some of the recipes in this book include wild mushrooms. Cooking and eating some species of wild mushroom can be dangerous. If you have any doubts at all about the species of fungus you have picked, do not eat it. Neither the publisher nor the author can accept any responsibility for the consequences of any mistaken identification of mushroom species.

I dedicate this book to my first grandson, Scott
Patrick, for being so appreciative when, at the
tender age of seven months, he ate three
helpings of his first solid meal, risotto, and for
his promising attitude towards the mushroom
world at eighteen months.

ACKNOWLEDGEMENTS

My deepest gratitude goes to the following family, friends and companies for having worked very hard in one way or another to make the publication of this book possible:

Roberto Bava; Peter Bazalgette; Silke Bruenink; Nina Burgai; Alessandro Carluccio; Priscilla Carluccio; Rosalba Carluccio; Gennaro Contaldo; Cassie Farrell; Luigi Ferrando; Gabriele Ferron; Richard Gay; Signora Giacobazzi; Jo Gilks; Giorgio Gioco; Giorgetto Giugiaro; Laura Giugiaro; Heather Holden-Brown; Graham Kirk; Giuseppina (Pinuccia) Novara; Helen Payne; Frank Phillips; Renato Piccolotto; David Pritchard; Liz Przybylski; Bruno Roncarati; Count Carlo Maria Rocca; Natale Rusconi; Stefano Secoli; Olga Urbani; Doug Young; the Alessi shop, London; the Conran shop, London; Carluccio's shop, London; the Neal Street Restaurant, London.

CONTENTS

INTRODUCTION

During the last thirty or so years, I have had the opportunity to travel widely in most parts of the world and the good fortune to sample many ethnic cuisines. This is something I take seriously – firstly to satisfy my insatiable culinary curiosity and secondly to discover if there is a cuisine I might prefer to that of Italy.

However I have to admit that, despite all my travels, and although I much appreciate many different ways of cooking, Italian cuisine remains the one I feel most passionate about. The recipes and cooking methods my mother taught me and everything I have learnt during the last forty years, including that which I learned during my experience as a wine merchant, have reinforced my belief that Italian cooking is one of the best and most loved worldwide.

During recent visits to the northern regions of Italy, I have been excited to find that the cuisine has not been compromised or watered down by the temptation

to cut corners. It is true that, like everywhere else, the hectic pace of life in the big cities has dictated a faster way of eating without necessarily improving the quality of life. And it was with great relief that, on one of my journeys, I encountered the Slow Food Society which was started by Carlo Pertini in 1986 and has its combined central office and restaurant in the small charming Piemontese town of Bra. Although this society is neither political nor religious, it is attracting more and more worldwide attention. It simply encourages its members to enjoy thoughtfully and masterfuly produced food, in peaceful and tranquil surroundings, in the company of other like-minded people. We spend so much time running around trying to earn our daily bread – others run even faster to earn more than they can possibly use – that we often sacrifice the quality of life. This society invites you to take it easy – that's what I call civilization!

Today's Italian cooking has its origins in the struggle of the poor people of the last century imitating the culinary traditions of the rich and powerful. This came about because the poor, having feasted on the leftovers from huge banquets, could appreciate the extent to which the rich would go to satisfy their appetites and promote their status. The peasants, in trying to share these pleasures, had to be very inventive with what they had – which was often very little indeed. They made use of what grew wild and could be collected free, and today, the tables have turned! The peasants' ingredients of dandelion, *rucola* (rocket), oregano, mint, tops of hops, wild asparagus and all sorts of *funghi* now command a very high price because of their rarity and their taste. The ingredients once used by the poor have become those sought by the rich, and they now form the basis of many contemporary mouthwatering specialities! The good news is that if you know about wild food, then you can still collect it free when enjoying a pleasant walk in the country.

Italian cuisine evolved from the influences of Roman imperialism followed by the invasion of Normans, Barbarians, Goths, Vizigoths and Gauls and Slavs from the East, as well as from Southern civilizations like the Greeks, Arabs, Etruscans and Saracens. Commerce thrived when the four sea ports of Venice, Genova, Pisa and Amalfi, the so-called *repubbliche marinare*, began to import special spices from the Middle East. Saffron, for instance, was used as a currency and ensured that Italian cuisine had an exotic side which was developed by the Venetians and Tuscans and then exported to the rest of Europe, coming to rest in France where it became the famous *haute cuisine*. The benefits of the discoveries made by explorers, including Columbus, were incorporated into Italian cooking and so ingredients such as the tomato and the potato became essential to it. It is this way that food travels and cultures exchange cuisines which intrigued me years ago and made me determined to become the 'apostle' of Italian food abroad.

Every aspect of Italian food, rich or poor, is part of the culture and should be preserved while still allowing for contemporary innovation. Our modern way of life, with all its technological aids, allows us to feed large numbers of people, but this is done at a cost in terms of taste, flavour and texture. Although freezing can be used to preserve food, it does not transform it in the way that, in the past, preserved pork became salami and milk became cheese. Food is preserved today merely for the sake of the logistics of distribution. Sadly, along the way it may lose its original taste, texture, fragrance and sensuality.

The delights of the full panorama of northern Italian food are embraced in this book. It was researched with knowledgeable people I knew would produce outstanding food in the traditional manner. I hope this book will give you an idea of what authentic Italian food is really about. Some of the recipes and ideas are created by me, some are taken with the generous permission of people I have met on my travels.

All Italians *love* to eat well. You do not need a lot of money to enjoy good Italian food. What you need is imagination, knowledge, a little patience for preparation and enough of a desire to live happily and healthily. This, I believe, is the Italian culinary philosophy.

The aim of this book is to help you achieve this by presenting traditional recipes from a contemporary and practical point of view, enabling you to enjoy the taste and quality of food we know existed in the past and we would like to remember. I hope you will have lots of fun preparing what is, in my experience, one of the best cuisines in the world.

ANTONIO CARLUCCIO

THE LARDER

Of all the so-called necessary items one has to stock in the larder to avoid being
'unprepared', there are many things I end up throwing away because they are
never used. I must admit, however, that I am like a hamster and tend to hoard
things. To cook Italian food there are not many items you always must have,
because Italian cooking is based on fresh ingredients. These are more or less
the only ingredients I would suggest you need.

FATS AND OILS

We use both butter and olive oil on a daily basis. Butter tends to be used more
in the north of Italy and is always unsalted. It can be simply stored in the fridge
but of course you should watch the sell-by date. In addition, I suggest you stock
at least three different oils which, with the recent influx of oils onto the market,
is not difficult to achieve.

Firstly, a seed oil, like sunflower oil, is good for frying. If you have to fry fish or other food which has an unmistakable taste and smell, it is preferable to use oil which you can discard after use. Secondly, a pure olive oil should be used for the base of sauces and for frying certain foods where you want to retain the sweet taste of olives. Thirdly, you should keep a really good extra virgin olive oil. Italian is best because you can rely on it being really virgin and because of its aroma, typical of the area it comes from. The further south you go in Italy, the more intense the oil becomes in taste and texture. However, good-quality extra virgin olive oil should not be used in cooking as this flavour is lost. This type of oil is ideal eaten raw on salads or as a condiment on warm food.

Do not keep oil for a long time. If you do not use a lot, buy smaller bottles.

VINEGARS

I keep a good *aceto di vino rosso*, Chianti red wine vinegar, for use on salads and in sauces or marinades. Balsamic vinegar is more difficult to choose because the various types vary in quality and so the price ranges from moderate to very expensive. The most expensive is *aceto balsamico tradizionale di Modena*. This is a very special vinegar which is left to age for 40 or even 50 years. It is used by the drop on very delicate steamed fish dishes, on raw meat or grilled white meat. It can also be eaten on a piece of Parmesan cheese and some people I know even enjoy it on its own by the spoonful.

There are other balsamic vinegars which are 5, 10 or 15 years old and these are not so expensive (but neither are they the cheapest which are probably not genuine) and although these cannot be called *tradizionale* they can be added to sauces, vinaigrettes and extra-fine marinades.

PASTA

I suggest that in your store cupboard you always keep a packet of short dried pasta such as *tubettini* or *farfalline* for soups or minestrone, a packet of spaghetti, a packet of larger shaped pasta, such as *conchiglie* and a packet of egg tagliatelle nests. When you have leftovers of different kinds of pasta shapes, this is ideal for making pasta and bean soup. Don't forget, however, to check the sell-by dates on the packets from time to time.

RICE

The best rice for making the traditional risotto is carnaroli, the Rolls Royce of rice. For Venetian risottos, the best is vialone nano. Arborio rice is also good and remember only these types of rice should be used for risotto.

POLENTA

For good polenta, you would use traditional *farina di polenta*. To cook it takes

40 minutes of constant stirring, which is what Italian peasants used to do every day. Nowadays you can buy 'quick' polenta, which is ready in 5 minutes and offers a good alternative. In either form, you should always keep a packet in the storecupboard.

'OO' FLOUR

This extra-fine flour is made from tender Italian wheat and is mostly used to make pasta. When eggs are added, it gives the cooked pasta the 'crunchiness' much desired by Italians. When they say *al dente*, they mean that after cooking, the pasta still offers a certain resistance to the tooth which, from now on, I shall call 'dentiness'. Commercially, pasta is made from durum wheat semolina. When this is of good quality it offers good 'dentiness' without using eggs. This semolina is also used in southern Italy for certain handmade pasta shapes.

TOMATOES

I have purposely not mentioned storing ready-made sauces since I have discovered that industrial sauces often contain too many herbs in an attempt to make them taste Mediterranean. The use of dried oregano or, even worse, dried basil, gives a repulsive, artificial taste to the sauce.

If you cannot get hold of fresh ripe tomatoes, it is better to keep some *polpa di pomodoro* in your storecupboard. This is the pulp of ripe tomatoes, which you can flavour with the seasoning of your choice.

Please, please do not use tomato ketchup on pasta! A few good tins of peeled tomatoes and tubes of tomato purée are always handy in the larder.

HERBS

The only dried herb I would keep is wild oregano and this is suitable only for certain sauces and not for everything. Otherwise fresh basil, fresh mint and fresh rosemary are always part of my culinary vocabulary.

SPICES

Of the many spices used in the past 500 years in Italy, only a few are still used in everyday cooking. Cardamom, ginger, cumin and many others were used during the Renaissance to give various dishes an exotic taste. Of those dishes, only one remains almost untouched: *panforte nero* from Siena. This is a cake from the Middle Ages which is also flavoured with pepper, cinnamon, cloves and nutmeg. These last four spices, together with saffron, are the ones I would recommend you keep in the larder.

The other spice which is vital in Italian cooking is the dried *porcino* or cep. The addition of just a few slices of this special very Italian dried *funghi* can alter beyond recognition sauces of any kind. Used as a spice and combined with fresh cultivated mushrooms, it will impart that very desirable musty flavour typical of wild mushrooms.

FRESH GARLIC, ONIONS AND SHALLOTS

These should always be available. They are an integral part of every sauce and dish and very handy because they keep for quite some time.

CAPERS

These are very important to Italian cooking as long as they are used sensibly. They are available both in brine and in vinegar, but I prefer the Sicilian ones from Lipari kept in salt.

They have a wonderful flavour and I would recommend you keep two sizes, very small to use whole and large to be chopped.

ANCHOVIES

Tinned anchovies are very useful to add to sauces, but I enjoy them in *salsa verde* or simply on a piece of buttered bread as a snack. The ones with the most flavour are the ones kept under salt, but these are not easily obtainable, therefore a quality brand of anchovy fillets in oil is a good alternative. In a similar way, tuna in oil can be very handy for quick improvised sauces or snacks.

PARMESAN

This should never be missing from an Italian larder. Parmigiano Reggiano is the best and can be kept in the fridge for quite some time wrapped in foil. I would suggest you buy a little piece at a time and always use it freshly grated.

LARDO

Years ago *lardo* was hanging in every Italian larder. It is a type of very thick salted and air-cured lard. Nearly every good sauce or dish started with a *battuto di lardo*, crushed cubes of the preserved pork fat cooked with oil and garlic or onions. It's a pity that this is disappearing. However, I always keep a piece of fatty *speck*, its counterpart from southern Tyrol, which can either be cut into thin slices and eaten on toast or used for flavouring sauces, soups and vegetables.

BREADCRUMBS

Good real breadcrumbs are necessary so you can turn a piece of fish or meat into a quickly fried meal.

COFFEE

Some Italian coffee should always be available. The end of an Italian meal would not be complete without a strong espresso!

ANTIPAS
appetizers

T I

The Romans were fond of the *antipasto*, the course that comes before the *primo* (first course). They used to eat things like preserved fish, such as anchovies, and shellfish washed down with a mixture of wine and honey. The point of this course is to titillate the palate and awaken the stomach to the pleasures to come. Its name comes from *ante* meaning before and *pasto* meaning meal.

A respectable Italian meal of any kind starts with at least a few slices of salami and some pickled vegetables. The more formal the meal, the more varied and interesting the *antipasto*. It is also a way of showing off the host or hostess's skills of special preparation and presentation!

Antipasti can be cold, using ingredients such as *affettati* (sliced preserved meats like salami, ham, *speck*, *bresaola*, and *culatello*); fish *in carpione* (marinated), smoked eel and trout, and anchovies in various guises; preserved vegetables such as *porcini in olio*, little artichoke hearts in olive oil, *cetriolini* (gherkins), peppers, aubergines and sun-dried tomatoes; or eggs, hard-boiled and filled with mayonnaise or set in aspic. Not to forget the whole range of *crostini*, toasted bread with wonderfully delicious accompaniments, from simply a tomato to a sophisticated pâté. Warm *antipasti* can be based on eggs, cheese and truffles, and such dishes are more in the French tradition.

Northern Italy enjoys a wide range of *antipasti* that certainly make the best use of local specialities and traditions, and Piemonte is considered to have the greatest variety. Some restaurants are renowned for their *antipasto* selection and, in such a place, I, for one, would definitely choose to indulge in lots of *antipasti* with, perhaps, a *primo* and a dessert, but miss out on the *secondo*. However with *antipasti* it's not the quantity but the quality that counts!

Previous pages: *Affettato Misto* (page 36); centre back – *Funghi sott'Olio* (page 37); centre – *Acciughe in Salsa Verde* (page 33)

CROSTINI DI FEGATINI
Chicken Liver Crostini

SERVES 4

2 tablespoons extra virgin
 olive oil

1 medium onion, finely
 chopped

300 g (11 oz) chicken livers

2 large sprigs fresh rosemary

2 tablespoons dry white wine

2 large anchovy fillets

½ tablespoon capers, drained

4 tablespoons chicken stock

Freshly ground black pepper

Sea salt

100 g (4 oz) unsalted butter

12 thin slices of crusty white
 Italian bread, 10 cm (4 in)
 in diameter

This recipe is so good that it is worth making double the quantity so that you have some in reserve – you can always use it for little snacks. Crostini *are a favourite appetizer which originates in Tuscany, where they use not only chicken livers but also game birds and wild boar to produce an enviable array of pâtés.*

Imagine you are leaning back on a wooden chair under a pergola in a hilly part of Tuscany, where you have one of those views of typical Italian landscapes painted by an Italian old master. In your left hand you have a fresh crostino *and in your right a nice glass of young Chianti. You have the right mix of ingredients to forget the cares of the world.*

METHOD

First, wash and trim the chicken livers. Fry the onion gently in the oil for 5 minutes until soft but not coloured. Add the livers and one sprig of rosemary and cook gently, stirring from time to time, for approximately 8 minutes until the livers are cooked. Add the wine and allow the alcohol to evaporate for 2–3 minutes. Discard the sprig of rosemary and coarsely process in a food processor. Be careful, this will only take seconds!

Return the purée to the pan. Add the anchovy fillets, capers and chicken stock and cook gently for 2–3 minutes. Check the seasoning, adding lots of black pepper but probably only a little salt, if any, due to the saltiness of the anchovies and capers. Finally, stir in the butter. Keep the pâté warm while you toast the slices of bread. Spread them with pâté, arrange on a plate and garnish with the remaining sprig of rosemary.

Antonio and friends truffle hunting in Umbria

INSALATA DI FUNGHI
Wild Mushroom Salad

SERVES 4

675 g (1½ lb) mixed *funghi*

6 tablespoons olive oil

**1 red chilli pepper, finely
  chopped**

2 garlic cloves, finely chopped

**2 tablespoons coarsely
  chopped parsley**

2 lemons

Salt to taste

Every time I return from a funghi *hunt with just a few bits and pieces, I enjoy this salad. It is delicious made with chanterelles or morels to which you can add a few cultivated shiitake, oyster or button mushrooms. Before picking wild mushrooms, always consult a reliable reference book (see page 208).*

METHOD

Bring to the boil a pot of slightly salted boiling water. Prepare the mushrooms by cleaning them and then discarding any tough and non-presentable pieces. Throw into the boiling water and cook for 5 minutes and drain them.

Meanwhile heat the oil in a pan and gently fry the garlic and chilli for a minute. Add the mushrooms, stir fry for a minute or so, add salt and the chopped parsley. Allow to cool. Serve with lemon halves and a sprinkling of parsley.

CARCIOFINI RIPIENI
Stuffed Baby Artichokes

SERVES 4

12 baby artichokes

Juice 1 lemon

FOR THE STUFFING

120 g (4½ oz) stale white breadcrumbs

150 ml (¼ pint) milk

1 tablespoon finely chopped fresh flat-leaf parsley

¼ garlic clove, crushed

1 tablespoon freshly grated Parmesan

½ tablespoon drained capers

Large pinch sea salt and freshly ground black pepper

Extra virgin olive oil

The origin of this recipe must come from the Jewish ghetto in Rome where kosher food was the rule. These are popular with a lot of my Jewish friends.

During cooking, the artichokes should be practically covered with olive oil but that is an expensive way of using the oil. Alternatively you can put 1 cm (½ in) in the bottom of the pan and then add sufficient water to push the level of the oil higher. This allows the temperature to be controlled more easily.

Three artichokes per person is a wonderful starter and they are very good as part of an antipasto.

METHOD

Trim the artichokes, cutting off the top third and trimming round the base to remove all the tough leaves. Cut out any choke, making a hollow in the centre which will hold the stuffing. Plunge into a bowl of water acidulated with lemon juice to prevent discoloration.

Meanwhile, soak the breadcrumbs with the milk and squeeze out the moisture with your hands. Mix with the remaining stuffing ingredients. Fill the artichokes with the stuffing and pack side-by-side in a pan. The size of the pan is important as the artichokes must fit closely together. Drizzle the artichokes with a thin stream of olive oil and fill the base of the pan with 1 cm (½ in) depth. Add water to within 1 cm (½ in) of the top of the artichokes. Cover with a lid and simmer for about 20–30 minutes until tender. They are cooked when a knife pierces the artichokes easily. Cool a little and serve.

MOSCIAME CON LE UOVA
Air-dried Fillet of Tuna with Scrambled Eggs

SERVES 4

8 free-range eggs

40 g (1½ oz) Parmesan

20 g (¾ oz) finely chopped parsley

Salt and freshly ground black pepper

4 tablespoons olive oil

20 g (¾ oz) butter

100 g (4 oz) very finely sliced *mosciame*

Mosciame di tonno *is tuna fillet, salted and air-dried, and this is how it used to be preserved for use when the tuna catch was less abundant. Today, this very expensive delicacy is thinly cut and normally eaten as an* antipasto, *sprinkled with lemon juice and olive oil. I created this recipe for my restaurant where it is very popular. If you can't get* mosciame, *you could use smoked eel or smoked salmon instead.*

METHOD

Beat the eggs in a bowl and add the Parmesan, salt, pepper and parsley. Put a frying pan on the heat with the olive oil and butter. Pour the egg mixture into the pan and stir quickly for a few seconds so it becomes scrambled but still fluffy and moist. Divide on warm plates and decorate with a sprig of parsley and the *mosciame*.

Eat as a starter. For a light main course increase the quantity of eggs and *mosciame*.

Following pages (clockwise from back): *Carciofini Ripieni* (page 24); *Insalata di Funghi* (page 23); *Mosciame con le Uova* (page 25)

INSALATA DI CARNE CRUDA
Raw Beef Salad

SERVES 4

275 g (10 oz) small end of the beef fillet, finely chopped by hand (or coarsely minced by your butcher)

Baby artichoke, sliced

Flat-leaf parsley to garnish

Toast or *grissini*

FOR THE MARINADE

Juice 1 lemon

4 tablespoons extra virgin olive oil

2 heaped teaspoons finely chopped fresh flat-leaf parsley

¼ small garlic clove, crushed and finely chopped

Sea salt

Freshly ground black pepper

This is very much a Piemontese speciality which is prepared usually the day before it is to be eaten and served as part of an antipasto *on bread or* crostini. *Don't worry about it being raw. The beef, after the preparation, will be perfectly 'cooked' by the acidity of the lemon juice marinade. This macerates the meat and allows the garlic flavour subtly to infuse into it.*

METHOD

Mix the beef with the marinade ingredients, cover with clingfilm and marinate overnight in the fridge. The acidity of the lemon juice will change the meat's colour.

To serve, arrange on a plate, decorate with a slice of raw baby artichoke and a small sprig of fresh flat-leaf parsley and accompanied either by toast or *grissini*, or serve in the middle of *Carne all'Albese* (see opposite).

CARNE ALL'ALBESE
Raw Beef Alba-style

SERVES 4

400 g (14 oz) medallions of very lean beef fillet

8 tablespoons extra virgin olive oil

4 tablespoons lemon juice

Salt and pepper to taste

Thin slices of Parmesan

Asparagus tips, thinly sliced, or thinly sliced white truffle

There are various raw beef dishes, mostly called carpaccio. *However, this recipe was created before that! Traditionally it is served with thinly sliced white Alba truffle which is available only between October and January. This is the summer version which uses asparagus though it is still called* Carne all'Albese.

METHOD

Place each medallion between sheets of clingfilm and beat with a mallet until thin. Layer the thin slices of beef to cover a plate. Top with the olive oil, lemon juice, salt and pepper and thin slices of Parmesan. Add the thin slices of asparagus or truffle and in the middle, if you like, a couple of spoonfuls of *Insalata di Carne Cruda* (see opposite).

Burano, Venice

INSALATA DI MARE DELLA LAGUNA
Laguna Seafood Salad

SERVES 6

1.5 kg (3 lb) mussels

550 g (1¼ lb) razor shells

1.5 kg (3 lb) clams

8 tablespoons extra virgin
olive oil

1 garlic clove, finely chopped

3 tablespoons coarsely
chopped parsley

Salt and freshly ground black
pepper to taste

400 g (14 oz) small squid

3 or 4 small octopus

550 g (1¼ lb) cuttlefish

400 g (14 oz) raw tiger
prawns

400 g (14 oz) scallops, shelled

1 bunch of spring onions

Juice of 2 lemons

In Venice I found the greatest choice of seafood I have ever seen for this dish. The method is relatively easy to follow, but the availability of different types of seafood could provide some problems. You can substitute some of the ingredients mentioned with other available types of fish – the important thing is freshness.

METHOD

Clean the mussels, razor shells and clams and put in a pan with 2 tablespoons of the olive oil, garlic and parsley. Cover with a lid and cook until all the shells have opened and the flesh can be taken out easily. Discard the empty shells and any others which haven't opened and strain off the juice. Clean the squid, octopus and cuttlefish well, removing the ink from the inside of the cuttlefish (see page 144). Wash well and boil for about 10–20 minutes or until tender. In a separate pan, put the prawns in boiling water for 6–7 minutes and the scallops for about 3–4 minutes. Peel the prawns. When all the fish is cooked, drain and mix together in a large bowl. Allow to cool. Slice the spring onions very finely and add to the bowl.

Make a dressing from the juice of the cooked mussels, lemon juice, the remaining olive oil, salt and pepper and mix with the fish. Garnish with some empty shells as artistically as you like!

LAVARELLI IN CARPIONE
Fish 'in Carpione'

SERVES 4

4 x 250 g (9 oz) freshwater fish

Plain white flour for dusting

175 ml (6 fl oz) olive oil, to fry the fish

2 carrots, finely diced

1 large red onion, finely chopped

2 sticks of celery, finely diced

120 ml (4 fl oz) olive oil, to fry the vegetables

4 glasses of red wine

8 tablespoons white wine vinegar

1 tablespoon whole peppercorns

10 bay leaves

1 tablespoon juniper berries

Salt to taste

When fishermen on Lake Garda catch large quantities of a fish called carpione they prolong its use by keeping it in a marinade of the same name. This marinade gives flavour to a rather delicate fish which can then be eaten as an antipasto.

You can marinate fish like eel, trout and other freshwater fish in carpione. *It is ideal in summer when the sun is strong and one does not want to eat too much.*

METHOD

Clean, salt and dust the fish with flour and fry in the oil until each side is crispy. Put in a ceramic container.

In a clean pan fry the vegetables in the oil for about 5 minutes. Add the red wine, vinegar, peppercorns, bay leaves and juniper berries and simmer for another couple of minutes. Pour over the fish while still warm and set aside to cool. Marinate in the fridge for 2–3 days before eating.

ACCIUGHE IN SALSA VERDE
Anchovies in Green Sauce

SERVES 6

300 g (11 oz) anchovy fillets, cleaned weight

200 g (7 oz) finely chopped fresh parsley

2 whole chillies, finely chopped

2 garlic cloves, finely chopped

1 tablespoon capers, finely chopped

4 small gherkins, finely chopped

Sufficient olive oil for covering

This was the contribution of my elder sister, Grazia, to a family reunion meal in Ivrea, and it is a very typical Piemontese speciality which is delicious either as part of an antipasto or as a snack for when you feel a little peckish. It requires a little work, filleting salted anchovies, to get the best taste, so it is better to prepare enough to enjoy for some time. Of course you can use tinned fillets of anchovies in oil. In this case, it takes only a minute to make as much as you want.

To make it even quicker to prepare, simply place all the ingredients in a liquidizer and blend until smooth. This makes a creamy consistency, but I prefer the texture of the method below. In either case it is delicious, but always serve it with plenty of fresh bread to dilute the saltiness.

METHOD

Fillet the anchovies, if necessary. Combine the parsley, chillies, garlic, capers and gherkins with the olive oil. Take a china bowl and build alternate layers of anchovies and the green herb sauce until it is all used up. Chill until required.

If the oil congeals in the fridge, don't worry as it will melt again once the dish is taken out.

Following pages: *Insalata di Mare della Laguna* (page 31)

AFFETTATO MISTO
Mixed Preserved Meat

SERVES 4

300 g (11 oz) mixed cooked hams and salamis (such as Milano, Napoli, *culatello*, *salsiccia*, *calabra*, *capicallo*, *prosciutto*, *speck*, *bresaola* and *mortadella*)

In the past, the preservation of meat prolonged the use of slaughtered animals, especially pigs which were made into salami and hams. Now that we all have fridges and freezers and the need for preservation is no longer so vital, salami, hams and preserved meats are made simply because they are delicious either as a snack or, as we eat them in Italy, especially in the North, as an antipasto.

They are enriched by a few pickles, like the preserved mushrooms opposite, and eaten with grissini.

METHOD

Arrange the meats on individual plates, overlapping the slices and serve with some pickles of your choice and accompanied by *grissini*.

FUNGHI SOTT'OLIO
Preserved Wild Mushrooms

MAKES 2 x 500 g (1 lb) JARS

1.5 kg (3 lb) very fresh funghi (*porcini*, bay boletus, honey fungus, chanterelle, shiitake, button mushrooms or a mixture of all these)

1 litre (1¾ pints) white wine vinegar

500 ml (18 fl oz) water

20 black peppercorns

10 bay leaves

2 garlic cloves

5 cloves

Sufficient olive oil (not virgin) to cover

20 g (¾ oz) salt

Italians very much enjoy pickled funghi *with their* antipasto. *There is almost no family that does not get hold of at least a small quantity of wild mushrooms, especially if they are* porcini, *to preserve and enjoy at Christmas. If you want to pick your own wild mushrooms, you should always consult a good reference book first (see page 208).*

METHOD

Clean the mushrooms and discard any that have maggots. Cut large ones into quarters. Bring to the boil the vinegar and the water in a stainless steel pan, add the peppercorns, bay leaves, salt, garlic and cloves and let it boil for 5–6 minutes. Add the mushrooms and boil for another 10 minutes.

Take off the heat and remove the mushrooms, using a perforated spoon. Spread them on a very clean cloth to dry and cool. Do not touch the mushrooms with your hands to avoid contaminating them with bacteria. Place in sterilized jars and add sufficient olive oil to cover them. Make sure there are no air bubbles in the oil. Seal with a screw top or other lid and put away for at least a couple of months in a cool dark place.

PRIMI
first courses

Generally speaking, Italian cuisine is best known for its universally popular *primi piatti* (first courses) such as rice dishes, pastas and soups. The golden rule for a well-balanced meal is to alternate light and heavy courses, hot and cold, to take advantage of the full range of content, taste and texture. The visual side is also important, but secondary. In Italy we say *anche l'occhio vuole la sua parte*, 'the eye too wants to participate'.

From Northern to Southern Italy, there are hundreds of *primi*, all mouth-wateringly different according to the availability of local ingredients, habits, history and culture. For example, all over the Po Valley, water comes from the mountains to irrigate the rice fields of Vercelli and Novara in Piemonte, Pavia in Lombardy, and Padova in Veneto. Not surprisingly, the speciality of Milan, the rice capital of Italy, is risotto with saffron; in Vercelli it is a risotto with borlotti beans called *panissa*; in Novara, risotto is made with frogs; in Bergamo and other valleys, it is eaten with wild mushrooms; and in Venice with fish. In Alba, the rice receives the most precious of all toppings – white truffle. All these specialities are different, all extremely tasty and all use the best local ingredients.

Pasta came to the North this century, imported from the South where it has always been very popular. In Liguria, at the end of the last century, the Agnesi family was making pasta and even importing durum wheat from Turkey with its own ships. I am often asked whether fresh pasta is better than dried. The answer is that they can both be very good, provided they are made with the right ingredients.

Pasta is a complete form of nutrition, mostly based on carbohydrates but also

Previous pages (from left): *Ravioli di Rosalba* (page 64); *Spaghetti alla Pinuccia* (page 60); *Pansotti al Preboggion* (page 67)

including important trace elements. The digestive system breaks it down slowly, distributing the energy over a long time which it why all athletes are so fond of it. If well cooked, without too many rich and fattening sauces or other additions, pasta is the perfect meal which leaves the appetite satisfied for longer than many other foods. In any guise, pasta is wonderful. The proof is that there are few children (and children can be very fussy indeed) who do not adore it.

Primi also include lots of satisfying soups and broths based on rice, pasta and vegetables. Minestrone is a typical example that is cooked in so many temptingly different ways with a great variety of ingredients. Gnocchi, which is made with flour and potato, is also used in endless tasty first-course combinations. Polenta, likewise, can be used as a first course, provided the quantities are kept small and the accompanying sauce is not too rich.

With so many possibilities, which in many cases can be a meal in themselves, it is easy to compose a menu for any occasion. Indeed, it is difficult not to overdo it when you still have a main course, cheese and dessert to come. All the same, for me the *primi* are the best part of Italian cuisine. They are extremely versatile and offer endless possibilities.

ZUPPA DI MELONE E PROSCIUTTO
Melon and Parma Ham Soup

SERVES 4

1 very ripe 1–1.5 kg (2¼–3
   lb) cantaloupe or charentais
   melon (orange flesh is
   essential)

Juice 1 orange

Juice ¼ lemon

½ teaspoon sea salt

½ teaspoon coarsely ground
   pink peppercorns

Sugar to taste

4 large slices Parma ham, cut
   into thin ribbons

This is a wonderful way to enjoy Parma ham and melon and not only for toothless people! It adds another dimension to summer eating. The combination of a little orange and lemon juice gives it a special spiciness and, in summer, this is one of the bestsellers in my restaurant.

METHOD

Peel and liquidize the melon to a coarse purée. Stir in the orange and lemon juices. Season with salt and pepper and add sugar to taste (this should not be necessary if the melon is ripe and flavourful). Mix in one quarter of the Parma ham and divide the soup between the four bowls. Sprinkle the remaining Parma ham onto the soup, with a final twist of the pepper grinder on top.

ZUPPA DI CARDI E POLPETTINE DI POLLO
Cardoon Soup with Chicken Dumplings

SERVES 4

120 g (4½ oz) skinned chicken breast

5 tablespoons freshly grated Parmesan

⅓ teaspoon garlic oil or ½ garlic clove very finely chopped

Pinch freshly grated nutmeg

1 tablespoon fresh white breadcrumbs

1 egg

1 teaspoon chopped fresh flat-leaf parsley

Sea salt

Freshly ground black pepper

275 g (10 oz) cardoon or celery sticks

1.2 litres (2 pints) chicken stock or a bouillon cube

1 teaspoon chopped fresh chives

Cardoon, a member of the thistle family, resembles a large head of celery and has long white fleshy ribs and silvery green leaves. It gives an extremely subtle taste to the broth. Like celery, the tender inner stalk is the best part of the vegetable, but you can also use the outer part with the stringy filaments removed. If you cannot find cardoons you can use celery instead.

METHOD

Mince the chicken breast with 1 tablespoon of the Parmesan, the garlic, nutmeg, breadcrumbs, egg, parsley, salt and pepper in a food processor. Using 1 level dessertspoon of mixture for each dumpling, form into little balls with the palms of your hands, making 10 per person.

Strip the cardoon leaves from the stems, then peel the sticks to remove the outer strings and cut into 1 cm (½ in) pieces. Bring to the boil with the stock and simmer, adding the chicken dumplings after 10 minutes, until *al dente*. Add the chives, divide between the bowls and sprinkle with the remaining Parmesan.

ZUPPA DI ERBE DEL CREST
Crest Herb Soup

SERVES 4

1 small onion

1 small potato

1 carrot

25 g (1 oz) stinging nettle

25 g (1 oz) sorrel

25 g (1 oz) white dead nettle

20 g (¾ oz) yarrow (if this is
   not collected in Spring, strip
   the leaves)

50 g (2 oz) dandelion (pre-
   boil for 5–10 minutes to
   remove the bitterness)

25 g (1 oz) watercress

25 g (1 oz) spinach, wild if
   possible

25 g (1 oz) butter

2 tablespoons olive oil

1 litre (1¾ pints) chicken
   stock, or vegetable stock

When my friend Nina, who lives in the Aosta Valley, wants a crafty soup made with real fresh greens, she just pops out to the fields in front of her house with a basket and returns with a collection of dandelion, wild sorrel, nettles and pimpernel, among many others, full of vitamins and other goodies because they grow organically high in the mountains (see page 50). But dandelion and nettles grow everywhere, so you can try this soup, too, with whatever wild herbs you can find in non-polluted places!

METHOD

Chop the onion, potato and carrot into chunks. Heat the oil in a pan and sauté for 1–2 minutes. Add the stock, bring to the boil and add all the herbs. Gently cook for 15 minutes. Add the butter and liquidize the soup until smooth.

Serve immediately in pre-warmed bowls with some croûtons. This is a vitamin injection!

ZUPPA DI CAVOLO VALPELLINENSE
Cabbage Soup, Valpellina Style

SERVES 4

675 g (1½ lb) Savoy cabbage

**200 g (7 oz) stale bread, cut
into cubes**

**275 g (10 oz) Fontina cheese,
cut into small cubes**

1 litre (1¾ pints) chicken stock

50 g (2 oz) butter

*What a wonderful (and economical) way of using leftover bread. Cabbage is
cheap, too. The other ingredients are very typical of the Aosta Valley and make
this a remarkable, simple and delicious winter dish.*

METHOD

Clean, trim and slice the cabbage. Boil in lightly salted water until
tender, then drain. Take a large saucepan and place over a gentle
heat. Put a layer of cabbage in the bottom while still warm, then
a layer of bread, then a layer of Fontina. Continue doing this until
the ingredients are finished. Gently press down the ingredients
with the ladle. Bring the stock to the boil and pour over the other
ingredients. Leave to soak for a couple of minutes.

Meanwhile, melt the butter in a small pan. While still foaming
pour it over the soup. Stir and serve hot.

Following pages (from left): *Trofie al
Pesto* (page 64); *Zuppa di Melone e
Prosciutto* (page 42)

RISO IN INSALATA CON TRE FUNGHI
Rice Salad with Three Mushrooms

SERVES 4

10 g (¼ oz) dried *porcini*

150 ml (¼ pint) tepid water

200 g (7 oz) risotto rice, carnaroli, vialone nano or arborio

1 small onion, finely chopped

2 tablespoons extra virgin olive oil

250 g (9 oz) mixed mushrooms, thinly sliced

1 tablespoon finely chopped fresh flat-leaf parsley

Sea salt

Freshly ground black pepper

FOR THE VINAIGRETTE

2 tablespoons extra virgin olive oil

Juice of ½ lemon

1 tablespoon finely chopped fresh flat-leaf parsley

2 tablespoons chopped fresh chives

Sea salt

Freshly ground black pepper

Salad is something you usually associate with summer. For this dish, you have to choose a lovely late summer's day because you want to use wild mushrooms which are in the main available from the beginning of August to the end of October. I use the best risotto rice ever, carnaroli, not for the creaminess for which it is famous and which is normally the reason for choosing it, but for the big big grains which, being very absorbent, swell up and remain slightly al dente.

For the mushrooms, you will need at least three different kinds, but you can use as many as you wish. At this time of year, you can find ceps, horn of plenty and oyster mushrooms but you should always check a reference book before picking them (see page 208). If wild mushrooms are not available, the best replacements are the cultivated shiitake, oyster and button mushrooms, with the addition of some dried porcini *for taste.*

METHOD

Soak the dried *porcini* in the tepid water for 15 minutes, then squeeze dry, reserving the soaking liquor.

Simmer the rice in a large pan of boiling lightly salted water until *al dente*. Drain and, if the starch still remains, rinse with a kettle of boiling water. Meanwhile, fry the onion gently until soft without colouring. Add the fresh mushrooms, soaked *porcini* and parsley, together with a little salt to help extract the juices of the mushrooms. Mix the rice with the mushrooms, adding 2 tablespoons of the soaking liquor for moisture. Mix the vinaigrette ingredients together thoroughly and stir into the rice. Adjust the seasoning and serve chilled.

POLENTINA CON SCAMPI
Polenta with King Prawns

SERVES 4

90 g (3 oz) instant pre-cooked polenta

675 ml (1⅛ pint) water

2 teaspoons finely chopped fresh flat-leaf parsley

1 shallot, finely chopped

50 g (2 oz) unsalted butter

3 leaves fresh basil

Chilli oil or finely chopped fresh chilli pepper to taste

12 x 65 g (2½ oz) uncooked king prawns, peeled

4 tablespoons dry white wine

Sea salt

Freshly ground black pepper

This dish is reminiscent of Venice where polenta and prawns are cooked in various different disguises though seldom together. All the same, they make a nice happy marriage.

The traditional way of cooking polenta requires almost an hour's constant stirring; here I have used instant polenta which makes this recipe quick and easy to prepare. You can make this dish equally successfully with a combination of prawns and king prawns, as in the photograph on page 49.

METHOD

Bring the water to the boil, add salt and pour in the polenta in a fine stream stirring until it thickens to prevent lumps forming. After 7–8 minutes, remove from the heat and add the parsley.

Fry the shallot gently in the butter until soft without colouring, about 2 minutes. Add the basil leaves, chilli and then the king prawns, frying briefly on both sides. Add the white wine and fry for 2 minutes to evaporate the alcohol. Season to taste.

Arrange 2 tablespoons of polenta in the centre of each plate and spoon the scampi and the sauce around it.

Nina Burgai collecting fresh herbs

POLENTA DI NINA
Nina's Polenta

SERVES 6

**400 g (14 oz) polenta flour
(instant will do)**

2 litres (3½ pints) water

20 g (¾ oz) salt

150 g (5 oz) butter

150 g (5 oz) Fontina cheese

**100 g (4 oz) freshly grated
Parmesan**

On a recent trip to Italy I saw my friend Nina, from Champoluc, a small town in the Aosta Valley. Her polenta is famous all over the area. This is not only because the ingredients like the butter and Fontina cheese come from her own cows and taste sublime, but because of her very orthodox way of making it. She recently modernized the kitchen in her hotel, but the old wood-fired heavy-duty cooker remains, probably just to make polenta which needs a traditional slow stove. It is served to everyone eating in her non-fussy hotel in a non-fussy way simply with the tastiest chicken, salsiccia *(pork sausage) or* coniglio *(rabbit) in tomato sauce. If you want to use pre-cooked polenta, follow the instructions on the packet.*

METHOD

Bring the water to the boil, add the salt and let it dissolve. Pour the polenta a little at a time into the boiling water and stir without making lumps. This is important in the first phase when you have to watch that your arms and hands don't get sprayed by hot boiling polenta because of the vigorous bubbling. Keep stirring all the time and after 40 minutes add the cheeses and butter. (The ideal polenta should, after 40–50 minutes of constant stirring, come off the walls of the pan, perfectly amalgamated with the other ingredients.) Keep stirring on a moderate heat and serve with meat, fish or mushroom ragù.

Should you have any leftovers of polenta, let it cool and solidify, cut it into slices and grill or fry. It is always delicious. Even without any accompaniments, *Nina's Polenta* is a substantial dish.

RISOTTO CON DUE CARCIOFI
Risotto with Two Artichokes

SERVES 4

4 x 50 g (2 oz) small globe artichokes (trimmed weight) or hearts from 4 large fresh globe artichokes

600 ml (1 pint) chicken or vegetable stock or a bouillon cube

1 small onion, finely chopped

4 tablespoons extra virgin olive oil

100 g (4 oz) unsalted butter

320 g (11½ oz) Jerusalem artichokes, peeled, thinly sliced

350 g (12 oz) risotto rice (carnaroli, vialone nano or arborio)

50 g (2 oz) freshly grated Parmesan

2 teaspoons finely chopped fresh flat-leaf parsley

Sea salt

Freshly ground black pepper

The combination of the two artichokes gives this risotto an extremely delicate flavour. It is suitable for anything from a piatto unico *(one-course meal) to one of the courses for an extremely elegant dinner party.*

METHOD

Cut each small globe artichoke, or the artichoke hearts, in half and slice thinly. Bring the stock to the boil. Meanwhile, in a separate pan, fry the onion gently in the oil and 65 g (2½ oz) of the butter until soft without colouring. Add the globe and Jerusalem artichokes and lightly brown over a moderate heat. Add a little stock and braise for 2 minutes. Add the risotto rice and stir until each grain is coated. Gradually add the stock until it is absorbed and the grains are soft but still have a bite to them. Off the heat, stir in the Parmesan, the remaining butter and the parsley. Check the seasoning and serve.

RISOTTO ALL'ACETOSA
Risotto 'Sophiesticated'

SERVES 4 AS A STARTER

3 tablespoons olive oil

75 g (3 oz) butter

1 small onion, chopped

375 g (13 oz) risotto rice
(carnaroli, vialone nano or
arborio)

1.5 litres (2½ pints) chicken
stock, or a bouillon cube

150 g (5 oz) wild or cultivated
sorrel, stems removed

50 g (2 oz) freshly grated
Parmesan

Sorrel leaves to decorate

I created this risotto in Italy on the day my niece, Sophie, was getting married in England. Because I thought it was especially delicious, I decided to dedicate it to her. I sent her a fax with the recipe and good wishes for the occasion. That's why it is called Risotto 'Sophiesticated'.

You may find wild sorrel during your early summer outings in the country, but cultivated sorrel is available from good greengrocers and supermarkets.

METHOD

Heat the oil and 40 g (1½ oz) of butter in a saucepan. Add the onion and fry until soft. Stir in the rice, coating with the oil and butter. Stir-fry for a minute. Add a couple of ladles of stock and keep the rest boiling in another saucepan. Continue adding the stock to the rice a little at a time and stirring with a wooden spoon. Do not add more stock until it is absorbed. Add the sorrel leaves and continue stirring until all the stock is absorbed and the rice is cooked. After 18 minutes, take off the heat, the rice should be cooked *al dente* and not be too dry. Add the rest of the butter and Parmesan and beat with a wooden spoon energetically to achieve a creamy consistency. This is known as *mantecare* in Italian. Serve immediately on individual prewarmed plates and decorate, if you wish, with a small sorrel leaf.

Any leftover rice, when cold, can be mixed with a beaten egg and a little more Parmesan. With wet hands, form balls a little larger than a walnut and deep fry until crispy. They are delicious and can be made with any leftover risotto. They are called *arancini* (little oranges).

RISOTTO CON LENTICCHIE E SALAMINI
Risotto with Lentils and Sausages

SERVES 4

200 g (7 oz) green lentils

400 g (14 oz) salamini (luganiga type)

1 bay leaf

2.25 litres (4 pints) chicken stock or a bouillon cube

1 small onion, finely chopped

5 tablespoons extra virgin olive oil

200 g (7 oz) potatoes, peeled and cut into 5 mm (¼ in) dice

2 sticks celery, washed and cut into 5 mm (¼ in) dice

2 carrots, peeled and cut into 5 mm (¼ in) dice

2 ripe tomatoes, chopped, or 2 tablespoons *polpa di pomodoro* (tomato pulp)

320 g (11½ oz) risotto rice (carnaroli, vialone nano or arborio)

Sea salt

Freshly ground black pepper

This dish is produced in various ways and is typical of the Vercelli area and Novara, the main commercial centre of Italian rice cultivation. Traditionally you would use rice from the last harvest and the first sausage made with a newly killed pig. They also make a very delicious version there with frogs, but I discovered they were very difficult to catch so here I have used little salamini instead.

This is a one-course meal, the quantity is abundant and it is a dish to enjoy on a day when you are really hungry. If you do not have lentils, you can use beans or chickpeas.

METHOD

Simmer the lentils, salamini and bay leaf in the chicken stock for 15 minutes, covered.

In the meantime, fry the onion gently in the oil until soft but without colouring. Add the potatoes, celery, carrots and tomatoes and fry gently for 2 minutes. Add the risotto rice and stir to coat each grain. Stir in 1 ladleful of broth, lentils and sausages to the rice at a time, and continue to stir, allowing each ladleful to be absorbed into the rice grains before more is added. Continue until all is incorporated, when the rice should be creamy but still retain some bite. Check the seasoning and serve.

Sorting lentils in Castelluccio

RISOTTO ALL'ISOLANA
Risotto Isola-style

SERVES 4

50 g (2 oz) butter

4 tablespoons olive oil

200 g (7 oz) skinless pork sausage, or lean pork mince seasoned with salt and pepper and a touch of garlic

1 medium onion, finely chopped

300 g (11 oz) vialone nano rice

750 ml (1¼ pint) chicken stock

1 teaspoon ground cinnamon

40 g (1½ oz) Parmesan

Salt and freshly ground black pepper

Gabriele Ferron lives on the border of the regions which produce carnaroli and vialone nano rice, between Lombardia and Veneto. He is not only a rice producer, but is renowned as the king of risotto and this is his recipe. He usually uses vialone nano, which is a shorter-grain rice, used typically in Verona and Venice. It is absorbent whilst remaining al dente, *so it is perfect for the very hearty dishes of the Veneto region. Carnaroli on the other hand is a longer-grain rice but it has equally absorbent characteristics and belongs to the Lombardia region. You can use either of these rice types here.*

METHOD

Heat 20 g (¾ oz) of the butter and 2 tablespoons of the oil in a frying pan and add the sausage or mince and fry until brown.

In another large pan, heat the remaining oil and fry the onion until soft. Then stir in the rice and coat for a couple of minutes. Add the chicken stock and leave to simmer for about 10 minutes with the lid on. Here it differs from the usual way of making risotto as all the liquid is put in at once and not gradually. After 10 minutes, add the meat, stir well and continue to cook for a further 8 minutes. Add salt and pepper to taste and the cinnamon. Take off the heat, add the remaining butter and Parmesan, and beat thoroughly for a minute. Serve immediately.

RISOTTO DI ZUCCA
Pumpkin Risotto

SERVES 4

2 tablespoons olive oil

90 g (3½ oz) butter

4 sprigs rosemary, 2 finely chopped and 2 whole

1 garlic clove, whole

600 g (1 lb 6 oz) pumpkin flesh, chopped into very small chunks

300 g (11 oz) carnaroli rice

1 small onion, finely chopped

1 litre (1¾ pints) chicken stock

50 g (2 oz) Parmesan

Salt and freshly ground black pepper

This recipe comes from the Hotel Cipriani in Venice, a very welcoming place though rather pricey! Its food, unlike that at many other 'international' hotels, reflects local eating habits, something I very much approve of. The pumpkin is very much undergoing a revival at the moment and Renato Piccolotto, the hotel's chef, cooks this wonderful risotto, which is as appealing to the eye as it is to the palate. It is very simple to make but, like all simple and delicate things, requires a little attention. Pumpkins are now widely available and can even be bought in chunks.

METHOD

In a pan, heat the oil and a third of the butter, add the sprigs of rosemary, garlic and the pumpkin. The pumpkin will automatically exude some liquid and so no water needs to be added. Cook for about 20 minutes or until the pumpkin softens and dissolves. Remove the rosemary sprigs and garlic clove.

In another large pan, heat half the remaining butter and fry the onion gently until soft, add the rice and stir-fry for a few minutes. Add a little of the chicken stock and then the pumpkin mixture. Add more stock until it is all used and absorbed by the rice, stirring from time to time to avoid sticking to the pan.

Take off the heat and beat in the remaining butter and the Parmesan and sprinkle with the chopped rosemary. If you have a spare pumpkin, deseed, warm inside with hot water, drain, fill with the risotto and serve.

Following pages (from left): *Risotto di Zucca* (page 57); *Polentina con Scampi* (page 49)

SPAGHETTI ALLA PINUCCIA
Spaghetti for Pinuccia

SERVES 4

400 g (14 oz) uncooked king prawns

6 tablespoons olive oil

1 garlic clove, chopped

1 medium-sized red chilli pepper, chopped

1 tablespoon fresh parsley, chopped

5 tablespoons white wine

400 g (14 oz) *polpa di pomodoro* (tomato pulp)

500 g (1¼ lb) spaghetti or fresh egg tagliolini

I created this recipe in honour of Pinuccia, the exceptional chef at the San Giovanni restaurant, in Casarza. I was incredibly impressed by her dedication in producing outstanding food with ingredients hunted personally on a daily basis. If you are in that area pay her a visit, it will be nicely rewarded.

You could use cooked king prawns here if you can't get raw ones and reduce the cooking time slightly. Also, if you use tagliolini (as in the photograph on page 40) the pasta will take slightly less time to cook.

METHOD

Peel the central part of the prawns, leaving the head and tail shell intact. Heat the oil in a frying pan and add the garlic, chilli and parsley, taking care not to burn them. Then add the prawns and fry for a minute. Stir in the wine and the tomato pulp. Cook for a further 2–3 minutes.

Meanwhile, cook the pasta in slightly salted boiling water. If using fresh, cook for 2–3 minutes, if using the dried variety about 6–7 minutes.

Drain the pasta, add to the pan with the sauce, mix very well and serve immediately.

RAVIOLO APERTO CON FUNGHI
Open Raviolo with Mushrooms

SERVES 4

10 g (¼ oz) dried *porcini*

Freshly made pasta using
   100 g (4 oz) strong white
   plain flour and 1 egg (see
   master recipe page 74)

65 g (2½ oz) butter

1 small onion, finely chopped

300 g (11 oz) mixed fresh
   wild mushrooms, cleaned
   and thinly sliced

1 tablespoon finely chopped
   fresh flat-leaf parsley

25 g (1 oz) ground almonds

6 tablespoons milk

Sea salt

Freshly ground black pepper

Following pages (from left): *Marille in Insalata* (page 71); *Raviolo Aperto con Funghi* (page 61)

Funghi – *I always have to think of something special to say because I really like them: picking, eating and, naturally, preserving them. In this recipe, they look as though they are having a wonderful rest under a blanket, but only until you have dug in with the fork!*

Use porcini *and chanterelles if they are in season, otherwise use mushrooms like the exotic shiitake, or button mushrooms combined with dried* porcini. *If using wild mushrooms, always consult a reference book first (see page 208).*

Here I use ground almonds rather than cream to achieve a smooth creamy sauce.

METHOD

Soak the dried *porcini* in 150ml (¼ pint) water for 15 minutes, then squeeze dry, reserving the soaking liquor.

Either roll by hand, or use a pasta machine, to obtain 8 flat sheets of pasta measuring 15 × 15cm (6 × 6in). Cover with a clean tea towel. Meanwhile, in a large pan boil plenty of salted water.

In another pan, melt the butter and fry the onion gently until soft without colouring. Add the fresh and soaked *porcini* to the pan, stirring, and fry for 2 minutes. Stir in the soaking liquor, parsley, ground almonds, milk, salt and pepper.

Simmer the pasta in the salted water until *al dente*. Drain and pat dry with kitchen paper. Place individual sheets on 4 warmed plates, spoon the mushrooms and their sauce on top (reserving a little for the final garnish) and cover with the remaining pasta sheets, folding the corner back, as if to prepare the bed for the night, exposing the filling. Add a little of the sauce and serve.

TROFIE AL PESTO
Trofie with Pesto

SERVES 4

4 garlic cloves

40–50 fresh basil leaves

10 g (¼ oz) coarse sea salt

50 g (2 oz) pine kernels

Extra virgin olive oil, as required

50 g (2 oz) freshly grated Parmesan

500 g (1¼ lb) dried trofie or strozzapreti or fusilli

Basil leaves, to garnish

The photograph which you can see on the cover of this book was taken on a day when the weather was perfect for capturing the Italian countryside. The combination of the beautiful day, the scenery and eating this delicious dish was a great pleasure for the eye, the palate and the soul.

Trofie *is a particular pasta shape from Liguria. It is usually home-made but you can find it in good Italian shops. Alternatively you can use* strozzapreti *or* fusilli *instead.*

METHOD

Put the garlic and basil leaves in a mortar and add the salt, which under the pestle and the power of your elbow will function as a grinder. Also add the pine kernels and reduce to a paste, slowly drizzling in some olive oil. Incorporate the Parmesan and continue to grind with the pestle adding enough oil to achieve a very smooth and homogenous sauce of a brilliant green colour.

Boil the pasta in slightly salted water according to the instructions on the packet. Drain, transfer to a pre-warmed china bowl and mix thoroughly with the pesto sauce. Decorate with some basil leaves and serve immediately. The sauce should cover each piece of pasta and there should be none left on the plate!

TAGLIOLINI CON TRIGLIE
Tagliolini with Red Mullet

SERVES 4

675 g (1½ lb) red mullet

3 tablespoons olive oil

1 garlic clove, chopped

1 tablespoon parsley, chopped

5 tablespoons white wine

250 g (9 oz) *polpa di pomodoro* (tomato pulp)

Salt

500 g (1¼ lb) fresh or dried tagliolini

Pinuccia, who cooks in the San Giovanni *restaurant in Casarza, was a fishmonger before becoming a fantastic cook and perfectionist, and she knows all the tricks of the trade, and above all she never compromises about the freshness of fish. How wonderful to know that you are in the hands of a real professional. The* triglie di scoglio *which were used for the dish I ate there were caught that same morning.*

METHOD

Scale, gut and fillet the fish and cut into 5 cm (2 in) strips. Heat the oil in a frying pan. Fry the garlic, half the parsley and all the fish. Add the wine, stir well and cook for a couple of minutes. Season with salt and add the tomato pulp. Sprinkle with the remaining parsley and cook for a further 2–3 minutes.

Bring a large pan of slightly salted water to the boil. Add the tagliolini. If you are using fresh pasta, cook for about 2–3 minutes. If you are using the dried variety, 6–8 minutes.

When cooked, drain the pasta and add to the sauce. Sauté for a short time on the heat to coat well. Serve immediately.

An Italian meadow of wild flowers and herbs

PANSOTTI OR CAPPELLACCI AL PREBOGGION
Filled Pasta with Walnut Sauce

SERVES 4–6

**300 g (11 oz) pasta dough –
see master recipe (page 74)**

FOR THE FILLING

**1 kg (2¼ lb) mixed wild
greens (see recipe
introduction)**

40 g (1½ oz) butter

Pinch of nutmeg

**40 g (1½ oz) freshly grated
Parmesan**

1 egg, beaten

Salt to taste

FOR THE WALNUT SAUCE

250 ml (8 fl oz) milk

1 garlic clove

1 sprig fresh marjoram

**2 tablespoons fresh
breadcrumbs**

100 g (4 oz) walnuts

Few pine kernels

500 ml (18 fl oz) olive oil

Salt to taste

Marjoram to garnish

Preboggion is a mixture of the wild greens and herbs that grow freely on the Ligurian hills and is used for filling the tummy-shaped pasta which is typical of the region. You can use a combination of wild dandelion, wild beet, wild marjoram, wild borage or any other edible greens you can find.

METHOD

First, make the filling. Cook the greens until soft and squeeze out as much water as you can. Put in a pan with the butter, nutmeg and Parmesan and mix together until the butter has melted. Let the mixture cool, add the egg and salt to taste and set aside.

On a floured surface, roll the pasta dough out to a thickness of 3 mm (⅛ in). Cut out 4 cm (1½ in) squares, putting a teaspoon of the filling in each square. Close to obtain a triangle. Take the top and fold over, then wrap the two other corners around your finger. This makes a similar shape to tortelloni.

Put the milk, garlic, marjoram, breadcrumbs, walnuts and pine kernels in a blender. Process until you obtain a smooth mixture. Add the oil a little at a time (as when making mayonnaise) and blend. Add salt to taste and heat very gently, then put on one side.

Boil the pasta in slightly salted water for 3–4 minutes. Drain and dress with the warmed walnut sauce. Decorate with a sprig of marjoram and serve immediately.

PIZZOCCHERI
Buckwheat Pasta

SERVES 10

500 g (1¼ lb) pizzoccheri pasta

300 g (11 oz) French beans,
   topped and tailed

400 g (14 oz) potatoes,
   peeled and cut into cubes

500 g (1¼ lb) Savoy cabbage,
   cut into strips

200 g (7 oz) butter

4 tablespoons olive oil

2 garlic cloves, sliced

Pinch of freshly grated
   nutmeg

300 g (11 oz) Bitto cheese, cut
   in small cubes

300 g (11 oz) Taleggio, cut in
   small cubes

100 g (4 oz) freshly grated
   Parmesan

Salt to taste

Freshly ground black pepper

Valtellina is a valley in the Italian Alps not far from Milan. It is famous for bresaola, *the thinly sliced air-dried beef which is served as an* antipasto, *pizzoccheri, the only buckwheat pasta made in Italy and Bitto, a delicious local cheese. Taleggio is a neighbouring valley, where the famous cheese of the same name comes from.*

I had great fun cooking this dish for the students of a fashion school in Milan who were preparing for their end-of-year exams. In exchange I received a series of outrageous and impractical aprons specially made for me that only a school with lots of imagination could invent.

METHOD

Boil the pizzoccheri, beans, potatoes and cabbage together and cook for about 18 minutes or until tender. Put the butter and olive oil in a pan and gently fry the slices of garlic, being careful not to burn them, then add the nutmeg.

Drain the boiled ingredients and build up in a preheated dish a layer of pizzoccheri and vegetables, scatter over some of the Bitto and Taleggio cheese cubes, and then some Parmesan. Repeat the layers until the ingredients are finished. Pour the foaming butter on top – the heat should be enough to melt the cheese slightly. Mix well, season and serve immediately.

This is a sensational dish for vegetarians.

RAVIOLI DI ROSALBA
Rosalba's Ravioli

SERVES 4

**300 g (11 oz) pasta dough –
see master recipe (page 74)**

FOR THE FILLING

**225 g (8 oz) roast pork, veal
or beef, finely minced**

200 g (7 oz) braised cabbage

1 egg

**50 g (2 oz) freshly grated
Parmesan**

50 g (2 oz) unsalted butter

12 sage leaves

*In the best traditions of Italian cookery, my sister-in-law, Rosalba, makes
handmade ravioli in the same way as every good, food-loving cook. However,
everyone has their own formula for the filling which varies enormously from
fish to meat to vegetables to cheese. This filling includes braised, leftover
cabbage. Try it, but please feel free to try any combination of ingredients.*

To make life easier, buy a Raviolatrice, *an aluminium tray which has
square moulds with a jagged border. These can be bought at any good cooking
utensil shop. The cabbage should be braised with a little oil and a very little
water in a closed saucepan until* al dente.

METHOD

Mince the meat and cabbage, adding the egg and half of the
Parmesan, and mix well together.

Roll out the pasta dough in a thin rectangular shape to cover
the raviolatrice, gently pressing down the dough into the moulds.
With a teaspoon fill each mould, then cover with another slice of
rectangular-shaped pasta. With a rolling pin gently roll over.
Remove each raviolo carefully and place on a floured surface.
Cook in slightly salted water for 3–4 minutes.

Meanwhile melt the butter in a pan, adding the sage leaves and
pour over the ravioli on individual plates. Serve with the
remaining Parmesan.

SINFONIA DEL MARE
Sea Symphony

SERVES 4

4 tablespoons extra virgin
olive oil

1 tablespoon onion, finely
chopped

1 tablespoon celery, finely
chopped

20 g (¾ oz) carrot, finely
chopped

25 g (1 oz) baby octopus,
cleaned

25 g (1 oz) baby squid,
cleaned

25 g (1 oz) baby cuttlefish,
cleaned

10 g (¼ oz) pine kernels

1 garlic clove, finely chopped

25 g (1 oz) prawns, cut into
small pieces

25 g (1 oz) monkfish, cut into
small pieces

25 g (1 oz) fresh salmon, cut
into small pieces

1 teaspoon capers, finely
chopped

2 tablespoons dry white wine

250 ml (8 fl oz) fish stock

25 g (1 oz) cooked fresh peas

1 tablespoon mussel flesh,
chopped

20 g (¾ oz) clam flesh

Half a chilli

10 g (½ oz) *bottarga*, grated

Salt

350 g (12 oz) dried penne

100 g (4 oz) fresh tomatoes,
seeded and cut into cubes

3–4 basil leaves

This dish, which takes quite some time to prepare, is the showpiece of Cavaliere Gian Paolo Belloni, Chef and Proprietor of the Zeffirino Restaurant in Genova. I never knew so many ingredients could work together so well to create such a superior pasta dish. Sinfonia del Mare, *although presented rather theatrically, was a very pleasant surprise! You can omit a couple of the fish varieties if you have trouble obtaining them.*

METHOD

Put the oil, onion, celery and carrot in a pan and fry for a couple of minutes. Add the baby octopus, squid, cuttlefish and pine kernels and cook for 3 minutes. Then add the garlic, prawns, monkfish, salmon and capers and cook for a further 2 minutes. Stir in the white wine and hot fish stock. Then add the peas, mussels, clams, chilli and *bottarga*. Check for salt and add if necessary. Cook for a further 2 minutes.

Meanwhile cook the pasta. Drain and add to the fish. At this stage add the tomatoes and basil. Please note that the tomatoes should be fresh and not cooked.

MARILLE IN INSALATA
Marille Salad

SERVES 6

500 g (1¼ lb) marille

6 tablespoons olive oil

350 g (12 oz) cherry tomatoes

20 g (¾ oz) fresh basil

1 tablespoon small capers

50 g (2 oz) black olives

**2 tablespoons coarsely grated
  Parmesan**

The Italian car styling genius, Giorgetto Giugiaro, was commissioned by an Italian pasta company to design an ergonomic, 'sauce-dynamic' pasta shape. According to him this was at a time when people were being encouraged to eat less pasta, so his aim was to design a shape that would hold a lot of sauce! He succeeded in creating on the drawing board a piece of edible sculpture which should certainly be included in the Agnesi pasta museum in Rome.

These two recipes produced by his personal chef, in salad and with vodka (see page 72) are both excellent. Here, I prefer to use Taggiasca olives, which are very small and black.

METHOD

Bring a large saucepan of slightly salted water to the boil. Add the pasta and cook for about 10–12 minutes until *al dente*. Drain and put in a serving dish to cool and dress with 2 tablespoons of the olive oil.

Chop the tomatoes and basil. Add the capers, olives, the remaining olive oil and Parmesan and mix well with the pasta.

Keep chilled until ready to use, but not for more than one day.

GIUGIARO'S MARILLE ALLA VODKA
Marille Giugiaro-Style

SERVES 4

400 g (14 oz) marille

40 g (1½ oz) unsalted butter

¼ small red chilli pepper, chopped

4 tablespoons double cream

25 g (1 oz) concentrated tomato purée, mixed with 5 tablespoons lukewarm water

1 tablespoon cognac

1 tablespoon vodka

Salt to taste

It didn't surprise me that Giorgetto Giugiaro would also create an outrageous sauce for his pasta design (see page 71). He said he only gave ideas to his personal cook, but I think that was the modesty of someone known for greater things! Although vodka is not normally part of the Italian culinary vocabulary, this sauce is very good indeed.

METHOD

Heat the butter in a frying pan. Add the chilli, double cream and tomato purée. Take off the heat and stir well. Stir in the cognac and vodka. Season with salt.

Bring to the boil a large pan of slightly salted water and add the pasta. When cooked, put the pan with the sauce back on the heat and bring to the boil. Drain the pasta, mix thoroughly with the sauce and serve immediately.

STRANGOZZI ALLA NORCINA
Strangozzi Norcia-style

SERVES 4

1 garlic clove

75 g (3 oz) butter

50 g (2 oz) white truffle

400 g (14 oz) strangozzi, fresh or dried

50 g (2 oz) Parmesan

Freshly ground black pepper to taste

Norcia is more or less the capital of the black truffle and when you say a dish is 'alla Norcina', you will probably find truffles in it. Strangozzi are a typical Umbrian pasta made from durum wheat flour and water. The ribbons offer a certain consistency even after cooking because of their thickness and their shape, which is more square than flat. Combined with something as delicate and noble as the truffle, the result is outstanding.

You can use tagliatelle instead if strangozzi are unavailable.

METHOD

Rub a frying pan with the clove of garlic cut in half to allow the juices to flavour it and then discard. Put the pan on a gentle heat with the butter and pepper. Thinly shave three quarters of the truffle into the butter and keep warm without frying.

Meanwhile cook the pasta in plenty of water for 10–12 minutes (or less if the pasta is freshly made). Drain the pasta, toss in the pan with the sauce, add the Parmesan and serve with a few shavings of the remaining quarter of truffle.

PASTA ALL'UOVO
Fresh Pasta

**MAKES ABOUT 450G (1LB)
PASTA**
**300 g (11 oz) durum wheat
flour or plain flour, or a
mixture of both**
3 eggs, size 3 or 4
Pinch of salt

This recipe is the basis for all types of home-made pasta.

The best flour to use is '00' made from very finely milled tender wheat. You may also need to add a little durum wheat semolina if you want to make special shapes like trofie.

Standard tagliatelle are made with about 6 whole eggs per kilo of flour, plus a little water if required. Sometimes, for example if you are making ravioli, pansotti or other filled pasta, you will want a softer more workable pasta dough and this can be achieved by using about 3 eggs and the necessary water to a kilo of flour.

The important thing to remember when making pasta is to work the dough well with a lot of elbow grease and then to rest it for an hour before using it. Then, once you have rolled and cut the dough to the required shape, leave it to dry for half an hour or so on a clean cloth.

Homemade pasta cannot be kept for long because of its egg content. You should not refrigerate it – the best thing is to freeze it, though this will of course have an adverse effect on the quality of the finished dish. Bought dried pasta is dried industrially for 12 hours in special machines.

Never add oil to the water when cooking pasta except for large squares of pasta like open ravioli. Never rinse pasta in cold water – if you want to cool it down and interrupt the cooking process, add a couple of glasses of cold water to the pot when you take it off the stove.

In the restaurant of the Slow Food Society, I had some quite sensational pasta made with 40 – yes, 40! – egg yolks per kilo of flour. When I jokingly asked if they were quails' egg yolks I was very firmly told no, they were from Slow Food quality chickens!

METHOD

Sift the flour on to a clean work surface (marble is ideal), forming it into a volcano-shaped mound with a well in the centre. Break the eggs into the well and add the salt. Incorporate the eggs into the flour with your hands, gradually drawing the flour into the egg mixture until it forms a coarse paste. Add a little more flour if the mixture is too soft or sticky and, with a spatula, scrape up any pieces of dough. Before kneading the dough clean your hands and the work surface. Lightly flour the work surface, and start to knead with the heel of one hand. Work the dough for 10–15 minutes until the consistency is smooth and elastic. Wrap the dough in clingfilm or foil and allow it to rest for half an hour.

Again, lightly flour your work surface, and a rolling pin. Gently roll the dough out, rotating it in quarter turns. Roll out the dough to a sheet 3 mm ($\frac{1}{8}$ in) in thickness. If you are making filled pasta, go straight ahead and incorporate the filling as in the recipes. If you are making flat pasta or shapes, leave the pasta on a clean tea towel to dry for about half an hour.

SALSA NAPOLETANA
Basic Tomato Sauce

1 medium onion, finely
  chopped

6 tablespoons extra virgin
  olive oil

400 g (14 oz) can chopped
  tomatoes

6 basil leaves

Sea salt

Freshly ground black pepper

This sauce, the simplest of all the tomato sauces, is also a base for many others. In Italy it is made with ripe, sweet tomatoes in season. As well as serving it with spaghetti, you can use this sauce for topping pizzas.

METHOD

Fry the onion gently in the olive oil until soft without colouring. Add the tomatoes and simmer gently for 10 minutes. Stir in the basil and salt and pepper to taste.

SALSA ALLE ERBE
Herb Sauce

SERVES 4

½ small onion, finely chopped

4 tablespoons extra virgin olive oil

100 g (4 oz) butter

1 garlic clove, finely chopped

25 g (1 oz) pine kernels

8 tablespoons very finely chopped mixed herbs (chervil, parsley, chives, basil, mint, sage, rosemary and fennel leaves)

2 tablespoons chicken or vegetable stock

Grated rind ½ lime

Sea salt

Freshly ground black pepper

This is my recipe for herb sauce. Please try it and vary it according to your taste, increasing one or other of the herbs, or taking away one altogether. The important thing is that you cook it to your taste. Like pesto, it can be used for a variety of savoury pasta dishes.

METHOD

Fry the onion gently in the oil and half the butter until soft without colouring. Add the garlic and pine kernels and fry for 2 minutes. Stir in the herbs, stock, lime, the remaining butter, season to taste and serve. Be quick as it is vital you do not 'cook' the herbs but just warm them up.

Following pages (from left): *Risotto con Lenticchie e Salamini* (page 54); *Tagliatelle al Ragù* (page 81)

SALSA DI FUNGHI
Mushroom Sauce

SERVES 4

25 g (1 oz) dried *porcini*
mushrooms or mixed with
dried morels

150 ml (¼ pint) tepid water

8 tablespoons extra virgin
olive oil

1 sprig fresh rosemary

1 garlic clove, finely chopped

400 g (14 oz) fresh
mushrooms (e.g. field,
hedgehog and oyster), cut
into bite-size pieces

Sea salt

Freshly ground black pepper

FOR WHITE SAUCE:

15 g (½ oz) butter

FOR RED SAUCE:

2–3 tablespoons extra virgin
olive oil

4 tablespoons *polpa di*
***pomodoro* (tomato pulp)**

1 tablespoon tomato purée

There are many versions of this sauce. I have written about some of them in my earlier books but over the years my taste has evolved. My love for funghi *has encouraged me to experiment with many kinds and I believe I have been fortunate enough to sample some of the most interesting varieties. Because the wild season is short, you may be obliged to use cultivated mushrooms, although these do not give the same depth of taste. Remember, you should always consult a reliable reference book before picking wild mushrooms (see page 208).*

Sauces, in my opinion, should not be too liquid but, as in this case, have a basic liquor accompanied by little chunks of mushroom. Below are two versions of sauces with mushrooms, one white and one red. Dried porcini *give each a wild taste.*

METHOD

Soak the dried mushrooms in tepid water for 30 minutes and squeeze dry, reserving the soaking liquor.

Heat the oil and fry the rosemary and garlic for 20 seconds. If you are making the red sauce, add the extra olive oil at this point. Add the fresh mushrooms and soaked dried mushrooms and continue to cook for 15 minutes, stirring from time to time.

For the white sauce, stir in the soaking liquor and the butter and cook for a further 15 minutes. Serve with pasta, rice or on meat *scaloppine.*

For the red sauce, stir in the *polpa di pomodoro* and tomato purée and cook over a moderate heat for a further 15–20 minutes. Serve with polenta.

RAGÙ BOLOGNESE
Bolognese Sauce

SERVES 4

25 g (1 oz) butter

2 tablespoons olive oil

1 medium-sized onion, chopped

250 g (9 oz) minced beef

250 g (9 oz) minced pork

6 tablespoons white wine

1 kg (2 lb) *polpa di pomodoro* (tomato pulp)

1 teaspoon concentrated tomato purée

Salt and freshly ground black pepper

One of the best known Italian recipes abroad, Spaghetti Bolognese *does not exist in Italy. It is something you will find in a restaurant run by non-Italians or by Italians not in touch with genuine Italian food. The real thing is called* Tagliatelle al Ragù *and comes from Bologna in Emilia Romagna.*

Genuine Ragù Bolognese *is a combination of at least two types of meat, like lean minced beef and pork, plus oil and butter, a little wine, an onion, plump ripe tomatoes and tomato paste. The sprinkling of freshly grated Parmesan perfectly crowns this very Emilian dish.*

METHOD

Heat the oil and butter in a pan and fry the chopped onion. Then add the meat and fry until golden brown. Stir in the wine, tomato pulp and tomato purée. Season with salt and pepper to taste. Cover with a lid and leave to simmer for about 2 hours stirring from time to time.

Serve with freshly cooked tagliatelle and sprinkle with freshly grated Parmesan, if desired, but purists like this dish without.

PIATTI INF
baking and frying

ORNATI
E FRITTI

Baking and frying food are relatively simple processes. The complicated part is preparing the ingredients to put in the oven or frying pan. In baking, hot air cooks the food; in frying this is done by oil, butter or lard. Italian cooking uses both techniques to produce different, temptingly delicious, regional dishes.

The traditional way of baking bread has, sadly, now been left to idealists and a few peasant people. These lucky individuals enjoy the challenge of preparing mankind's most ancient and basic food. The smell and fragrance of a freshly baked loaf is unforgettable, and the taste, especially if the oven is wood-fired, is so unbeatably delicious that you immediately want to eat a chunk on its own, undressed by anything else! Life without bread would be very dull indeed and Italians certainly endorse this by seeming never to enjoy a meal without it!

Italian meals are prepared with the appropriate quantity of bread in mind. For example, the saltiness of salamis and hams, or the sharpness of preserved vegetables, would be overpowering without bread, and the Tuscan custom for baking bread without salt is for that very reason. In Italy, the only foods you do not eat with bread are pasta dishes, risottos and polenta, but, even then, people often enjoy mopping up the good sauce left on a plate after eating spaghetti. This custom is called *la scarpetta*, the 'little shoe'. It is not good table manners, but everyone does it all the same.

Bread which comes from huge bakeries is usually pretty tasteless and boring, so now Italians seek out specialist bakers where they pay high prices to appreciate just how good the flavour and texture of bread can be. *Grissini*, thin handmade breadsticks, originally a speciality of Turin, are now very widely available and, together with *ciabatta*, they symbolize people's desire to

Previous pages: *Focaccia* (page 100)

experience the full flavour of good food. In my restaurant, we bake *focaccia* and *grissini* daily, much to everybody's appreciation.

La vita non e'fatta di solo pane ('You cannot live on bread alone') is an old Italian saying, but it is also true, especially in Italy, that most meals are inadequate without bread as it is such a perfect vehicle for other foods. Many other foods that are baked in the oven supply that 'something extra' – for example, *timbale* of pasta or vegetables, savoury and sweet tarts and pies, biscuits and, of course, pizza which has taken over the fast-food world.

Frying is epitomized by regional variations of *Fritto Misto* (mixed fry). For example, on the Italian Riviera, as in most Italian coastal areas, you will find a *Fritto Misto di Pesce*, usually named after the area that it comes from. *Fritto Misto Ligure* or *Fritto Misto della Laguna* are the best known. They are quite different from each other and use locally caught, small, tender fish, such as baby octopus, squid, shrimps and whitebait, dipped first in plain flour and then crisp fried. *Fritto Misto alla Piemontese* is made from various meats, liver, vegetables and even sweet *amaretti*, dipped in beaten egg, coated with breadcrumbs and shallow fried in butter. In other parts of Italy, the *Fritto Misto di Verdure* (vegetables) is popular, and for this dish I particularly like to use *funghi* (wild mushrooms) and small artichoke hearts.

Finally, in addition to the above there are deep-fried courgette flowers and *Fritelle di Zucchine* (courgette fritters), and I highly recommend you to try my childhood favourite – fried pizza (page 97).

Gennaro and Antonio enjoy the results of a successful *funghi* hunt

FUNGHI SALTATI ALL'APERTO
Wild Mushrooms Sautéd in the Open

SERVES 4

450 g (1 lb) wild mushrooms (like *porcini*, saffron milk cup or whatever you find on that day)

50 g (2 oz) butter or ¾ tablespoon olive oil

1 small garlic clove, finely chopped

Salt

After a funghi *hunt, one feels quite hungry. Provided you bring with you a camping gas stove, a frying pan, butter, salt and bread, the rest can be supplied by nature.*

If you are in any doubt about the mushrooms you are picking do not eat them! Consult a reliable reference book, otherwise it may be your last meal!

METHOD

After cleaning, slice the mushrooms and heat the butter or oil. Add the mushrooms and garlic and stir-fry for 8–10 minutes. Add salt towards the end of cooking to taste. Enjoy with good bread *al fresco*!

TIGELLE DI ROBERTINO CON LARDO
Bob's Pancakes with Lard

MAKES 16 TIGELLE

500 g (1 ¼ lb) plain white flour

10 g (¼ oz) fresh yeast

150 ml (¼ pint) milk

150 ml (¼ pint) water

Pinch of salt

Butter to grease

FOR THE FILLING

150 g (5 oz) *prosciutto crudo*

150 g (5 oz) pork fat

1 clove garlic

4 sprigs rosemary

Freshly ground black pepper

The enthusiasm of Robertino, a very cheerful farmer I met with his family near Modena, is still vividly in my mind. He had such a passion for eating his food that I believe he became a farmer just to ensure that he would be at the source of it. Everything produced on this farm was excellent, including the Nocino (see page 195) for which he is famous.

Tigelle are small double-raised and baked breads vaguely resembling pittas. They are served hot, opened and filled with a paste mixture of pork fat, salt, rosemary and garlic, or coarsely grated Parmesan cheese and balsamic vinegar. In the Modena area they have a special tool to cook these pancakes which resembles a waffle iron. Accompanied by sparkling dry Lambrusco this is a very moreish snack which can become a large main course!

If you do not want to make the tigelle yourself, you can still enjoy the filling with grilled pitta bread.

METHOD

Dissolve the yeast in 3 tablespoons of lukewarm water. Then add to the flour with the other liquids and salt in a large bowl and knead to a dough. Leave to rise in a warm place for about 30 minutes.

When risen, take small pieces of dough and roll into balls the size of walnuts. Flour a clean work surface and slightly flatten each ball with a rolling pin or by hand, making 5 cm (2 in) rounds, 1 cm (½ in) thick. Take a clean cloth or tea towel and sprinkle some flour over it, place the round pieces of dough on this and cover with another cloth. Set aside in a warm place and leave to rise for about 15 minutes.

Meanwhile take the special *tigelle* griddle and place on a hotplate or gas ring to heat. Turn the griddle pan to heat both sides. Once heated, open the griddle pan and rub the butter over each mould. Place the pieces of dough on each mould and close the pan. Leave on the heat for 2–3 minutes each side or until slightly golden brown.

Remove from the griddle pan and keep warm until all the *tigelle* are made. Slit the side of each *tigella* and fill with a little of the *lardo*. (To make the *lardo*, put all the ingredients in a food processor and blend to a pulp.)

MAKES 24 FRITTERS

750 g (1¾ lb) courgettes, topped, tailed and coarsely grated

¼ large garlic clove, crushed

3 eggs, lightly beaten

2 tablespoons freshly grated Parmesan

Sea salt

Freshly ground black pepper

Pinch freshly grated nutmeg

5 tablespoons plain flour

2 tablespoons finely chopped fresh mint leaves

Extra virgin olive oil for shallow frying

FRITTELLE DI ZUCCHINI
Courgette fritters

I made these once on the spur of the moment, together with other improvised fritters (see page 92) when friends arrived unexpectedly and I didn't have anything to serve with drinks.

METHOD

Mix all the ingredients together. Shallow-fry heaped tablespoons of the mixture in 1 cm (½ in) of hot oil until crisp and golden on both sides. Only turn over when a good crust has formed on the first side and work quickly because the salt added to the mixture will draw out the water from the courgettes. If this happens, add a little more flour, but only as a last resort.

Following pages (clockwise from back): Crostata di Pasqua (page 96); Frittelle di Zucchini (page 89); Fiori di Zucchini Ripieni (page 93)

FRITTELLE DI BACCALÀ
Salt Cod Fritters

SERVES 4

450 g (1 lb) salt cod, soaked, cooked (see page 141) and skinned

2 eggs

2 tablespoons plain flour

1 tablespoon milk

2 tablespoons chopped fresh chives

Freshly ground black pepper

Oil for shallow frying

You sometimes find these fritters in corner cafés in Venice. Venetians will briefly interrupt anything at any time of the day to drink an ombra *(see page 200) (a glass of white wine) and eat little snacks like these.*

METHOD

Break up the salt cod into small pieces, ensuring any bones are removed, and mix with the eggs, flour, milk, chives and black pepper to taste. Add tablespoons of the mixture to 1 cm (½ in) hot oil and cook until golden on each side. Drain on paper towels and serve immediately, decorated with lemon wedges.

FIORI DI ZUCCHINI RIPIENI
Stuffed Courgette Flowers

SERVES 4

120 g (4½ oz) spinach

135 g (4¾ oz) fresh ricotta cheese

4 tablespoons chopped fresh basil

3 tablespoons freshly grated Parmesan

2 eggs

Large pinch freshly grated nutmeg

Slice of 1 garlic clove, crushed

Sea salt

Freshly ground black pepper

8 courgette flowers

Oil for shallow or deep frying

There are two types of courgette flowers. The one sold with the little courgette attached is the female. However, if you know a farmer or a keen gardener who grows courgettes, go and see him as he may give you male flowers, which are the ones attached to a stem without the courgette.

I can still remember the face of Padre Emiliano, a very nice orthodox Catholic from Grotta Ferrata near Rome, when I invited him to come and eat some stuffed courgette flowers with me. I don't think he had ever eaten anything like them before. The expression on his face after tasting one or two was of complete beatitude.

After courgette flowers, we went on to eat gnocchi with Gorgonzola cheese and my tiramisù, *and later on, he had a huge steak as well! When I mentioned that he might perhaps have overdone it, he said with a smiling face that his work had been very hard that morning and that was his calorie reward!*

METHOD

Wash the spinach well, cook, and allow to cool and squeeze to remove excess liquid. Mix the spinach, ricotta cheese, basil, Parmesan, 1 egg, nutmeg, garlic, salt and pepper together well. Using a piping bag, three-quarters fill each courgette flower. Beat the remaining egg and coat each flower with it. Shallow or deep fry the flowers until golden. Serve at once.

Following pages (from left): *Pizza Fritta* (page 97); *Timballino Vegetariano* (page 101)

CROSTATA DI PASQUA
Easter Tart

SERVES 6

FOR THE PASTRY

100 ml (3½ fl oz) olive oil

100 ml (3½ fl oz) water

300 g (11 oz) plain white flour

FOR THE FILLING

3 medium-sized globe artichokes

250 g (9 oz) spinach

2 tablespoons olive oil

1 garlic clove

250 g (9 oz) radicchio

300 ml (½ pint) water

10 capers

2 eggs, beaten

75 g (3 oz) Parmesan

Salt and freshly ground black pepper

Beaten egg or milk to glaze

An irresistible Easter tart suitable to be taken on a picnic especially on Easter Monday when every Italian, or almost every one, goes to the country to celebrate Pasquetta.

METHOD

Preheat the oven to 200°C, 400°F, Gas Mark 6.

To make the pastry, first mix the oil and water in a bowl. Gradually fold in the flour and mix to form a dough. Knead a little, cover, and leave in the fridge for about 20 minutes. Then roll out on a floured surface with a rolling pin to a thickness of ½ cm (¼ in) and line a 20 cm (8 in) diameter and 8 cm (2½ in) deep fluted flan tin. With the remaining pastry, cut 6 thin strips about 1 cm (½ in) wide and 20 cm (8 in) long, and set aside.

To make the filling, first of all clean, trim and halve the artichokes and cook in slightly salted boiling water until tender. Coarsely chop the spinach and cook in slightly salted boiling water until tender.

In a large pan heat the oil and add the chopped garlic. Let it sweat for a minute or two, then add the radicchio and the water, stirring well. Stir in the capers and leave to simmer for about 8–10 minutes or until the radicchio is tender. At the end of the cooking time all the water should have evaporated. At this stage add the cooked spinach and artichokes and mix together.

Put the filling mixture in a bowl and leave to cool. When cool, add the eggs, Parmesan, salt and pepper and mix thoroughly. Fill the pastry case with this mixture. Place the strips of pastry across the pie making a lattice pattern, trimming the ends where necessary. Then, with your fingers press down the edges of the pastry to hold in the filling (see picture on page 90–91). Brush the strips of pastry with some beaten egg or milk and bake in the oven for 35 minutes.

Delicious served hot or cold.

PIZZA FRITTA
Fried Pizza

MAKES 6 X 20 CM (8 IN) PIZZAS

FOR THE DOUGH

500 g (1¼ lb) '00' or plain white flour

20 g (¾ oz) fresh yeast, or dry equivalent

Pinch of salt

Olive oil for frying

FOR THE TOPPING

Basic tomato sauce (see page 76)

50 g (2 oz) freshly grated Parmesan

12 basil leaves, to decorate

The one dish of my mother's I remember most is Pizza Fritta. *It was hugely successful in my home and although my mother was constantly frying she was happy to see the pleasure she was giving! If you try this, for a party, make sure your guests can come into the kitchen to keep you company otherwise you'll be in there alone all night!*

METHOD

Put the flour in a large bowl. Dilute the yeast in water and leave for a few minutes. Add this, the salt and a little more water to the flour to obtain a fairly soft dough. Cover with a kitchen cloth and leave to prove for 1 hour by which time the dough will have doubled in size.

Gently heat the tomato sauce. Meanwhile, take a piece of dough about the size of an egg, and roll it out on a floured work surface. Heat the oil in a pan and when it is hot, add the pizza and fry on each side until golden. Place on a plate and, whilst still hot, pour on a little of the tomato sauce and spread evenly. Add the Parmesan and some basil leaves.

These are very moreish!

FOCACCIA AL FORMAGGIO
Cheese Focaccia

SERVES 4

1 kg (2¼ lb) plain white flour

500 ml (18 fl oz) water

100 ml (3½ fl oz) olive oil

10 g (¼ oz) fresh yeast

20 g (¾ oz) salt

500 g (1¼ lb) Stracchino or Taleggio cheese

Olive oil for greasing tin and sealing

This is the speciality of Camogli, a small picturesque fishing village on the Italian Riviera which takes its name from the words ca moglie *– meaning, in local dialect, the houses inhabited by the wives. This is because the entire male population were always at sea fishing.*

With its generous cheese filling, Focaccia al Formaggio *is a great delicacy. It is like a large flat strudel – the dough is just as thin and elastic. The cheese used in Camogli is the very soft Certosino but Stracchino or Taleggio cheese can be used instead and these are more widely available.*

You can eat this at any time from breakfast to dinner. It is always delicious!

METHOD

Preheat the oven to 240°C/475°F/Gas 9.

In a large bowl, mix together the flour, water, oil, yeast and salt and knead into a dough. Knead by hand for about 20 minutes (or in a mixer for about 5 minutes) or until the dough is elastic. Leave to rise in a warm place for 30 minutes.

Grease a large baking tray with oil. Take half of the dough and on a floured work surface begin to roll out with a rolling pin. Then stretch the dough by hand to obtain a thickness of 3 mm (⅛ in). Place on the greased baking tray and dot with knobs of cheese.

Take the other half of the dough and roll out to the same size and thickness and place over the cheese, pressing down with the fingertips. Seal the edges and dribble some olive oil over the top. Bake in the very hot oven for 15 minutes or until it is crispy.

Sunset in Camogli

FOCACCIA

SERVES 4

FOR THE DOUGH

500 g (1¼ lb) strong white
   plain flour

15 g (½ oz) fresh yeast, or dry
   equivalent

300 ml (½ pint) lukewarm
   water

2 tablespoons extra virgin
   olive oil

10 g (¼ oz) sea salt

FOR THE TOPPING

5 tablespoons extra virgin
   olive oil

Coarse sea salt

Freshly ground black pepper

(Or chopped onions,
   rosemary or other herbs)

In my restaurant and also in our Carluccio's shop next door, it has become traditional to have focaccia made by Gennaro. He makes it with the best ingredients and everyone loves it!

This flat bread can be served with many kinds of food, and is irresistible just out of the oven, cut in two like a sandwich with a slice of mortadella *in the middle. Different varieties come topped with tomato, onions or herbs.*

METHOD

Preheat the oven to 240°C/475°F/Gas 9.

Sift the flour into a bowl. Dissolve the yeast in the water and pour into a well in the middle of the flour, along with the oil and salt. Mix until a dough is formed and knead for about 10 minutes, until springy to the touch. Alternatively, mix all the ingredients in a food processor and, using the dough accessory, knead the bread for 2 minutes. Put into a bowl, cover with a damp tea towel and leave to prove for about 1 hour until it has doubled in size.

Knead the bread again to knock out any air bubbles and flatten out to an oval shape with your hands until 2.5 cm (1 in) thick. With the knuckles of your fingers press into the surface of the dough at 2.5 cm (1 in) intervals. Sprinkle with half the olive oil, then spread it gently over the surface with your finger tips. Sprinkle with salt and pepper or onions and herbs. Leave to rise again for about 30 minutes. Bake in the very hot oven for about 15 minutes until the base sounds hollow when tapped. Remove from the oven and sprinkle with the remaining oil.

TIMBALLINO VEGETARIANO
Vegetarian Timbale

SERVES 4

120 g (4½ oz) broccoli florets

90 g (3½ oz) French beans

2 x 200 g (7 oz) courgettes, cut lengthwise into 5 mm (¼ in) slices

1 x 500 g (1 lb 2 oz) aubergine, cut lengthwise into 5 mm (¼ in) slices

4 tablespoons seasoned plain flour

4 eggs, beaten

Olive oil for shallow frying

500 g (1 lb 4 oz) basic tomato sauce (see page 76)

200 g (7 oz) Fontina or Gruyère cheese, cut into 1 cm (½ in) dice

100 g (4 oz) freshly grated Parmesan

The traditions of vegetable cookery in Italy are the result of using regionally grown produce in a way which could replace meat in times when it was scarce and expensive. The result was that people in Italy now do not miss meat because there is such a wonderful range of vegetable dishes!

You may increase the quantities of vegetables in this dish and serve it as a main course if you wish. The quantities here make a wonderful starter.

METHOD

Preheat the oven to 200°C/400°F/Gas 6.

Cook the broccoli and French beans in boiling salted water, drain and refresh in cold water. Dry the broccoli florets on kitchen paper and slice. Cut the beans into 7.5 cm (3 in) pieces.

Dust the courgette, aubergine and broccoli slices with the seasoned flour, patting off any excess, dip in beaten egg and shallow fry in 2.5 cm (1 in) of very hot oil until golden brown on both sides. Drain on kitchen paper.

Into an ovenproof dish put 3 tablespoons of tomato sauce, then layers of aubergine, Fontina or Gruyère cheese, tomato sauce, Parmesan, French beans, courgette, broccoli, tomato sauce, Parmesan and then repeat the layers, ending with a layer of tomato sauce and Parmesan.

Bake for approximately 30 minutes until sizzling.

SECOND
main courses

Although Italians enjoy a wide variety of meat, it is rarely the focal point of a traditional meal. As a child I remember how happy we were on Sundays when we could eat roast chicken, knowing that whatever remained would be used to make a stock for a flavourful soup. During the Second World War, Italians were introduced to canned meat that came from the United States of America. This is still made by Simmenthal today. Recently I opened a can and thoroughly enjoyed the contents sliced and dressed with very thin slices of raw onion and a little oil and vinegar. It really did bring back many fond memories . . .

In my childhood, special cuts of beef could only be afforded by well-off families. The alternatives were pork, which could be eaten immediately or preserved as sausages, salami and ham (Parma being the best-known), lamb and goat. As a result, there are literally hundreds of Italian regional recipes for cooking lamb and goat, and these were the traditional ingredients of Easter feasts. After the war, beef became a measure of wealth and social status and grand ladies asked the butcher for *una fettina*, a little slice of pale tasteless veal.

With new methods of raising animals and increased standards of living, the Sunday roast chicken became very common indeed as did duck, goose, and *cacciagione* (game), especially at Christmas. Game in Italy has always been an important source of meat, but now it became even more so as it offered an alternative to farmed meat. Italians have always been mad about hunting, so much so that hunters have often shot each other, and the government was obliged to introduce safety regulations.

Today Italy is able to produce very good-quality meat of all kinds. In the Val di Chiana, near Florence, for example, they raise a small quantity of

Previous pages: *Brasato al Nebbiolo* (page 125)

exceptional quality beef which is very sought-after and a *fiorentina* (Tuscan T-bone steak) is something worth dreaming about. It's worth the journey to experience it yourself! Piemonte and Lombardy also produce excellent meat because the pastures of the slopes of the Pre-Alps are as fertile as could be. Because the Italians only want to eat good-quality meat, some beef is also now imported from Scotland. Rabbit, rediscovered as a regional speciality, and other game is popular in Tuscany, Liguria and Piemonte – all regions where there are plenty of woods and forests.

For Italian meals, the meat is prepared and cooked in a great variety of ways – stewed, roasted, fried, barbecued, braised and boiled. It is also included in sauces and even sometimes served raw. Because Italian meals are generally made up of several courses, it is not necessary to have large quantities of meat at any one time as you might in, say, Germany, Scotland or America. For this reason, Italians invented the *scaloppine*. Take a tender piece of veal, pork, lamb, chicken or turkey, beat it flat with a mallet, dust with plain flour and cook briefly in oil or butter, adding a little taste of Marsala, lemon, white wine or vinegar as desired. This epitomizes Italian cooking – fresh, fast, non-fussy and exceedingly tasty.

SPIEDINO DI NOCCIOLE D'AGNELLO
Lamb Nuggets on a Skewer

SERVES 4

250 g (9 oz) Jerusalem artichokes, peeled weight

450 g (1 lb) lamb fillet, cut into 5 cm (2 in) cubes

15 g (½ oz) butter

1 teaspoon plain flour

FOR THE MARINADE

½ garlic clove, sliced

1 fresh red chilli pepper, sliced

4 tablespoons extra virgin olive oil

1 teaspoon chopped fresh mint

1 teaspoon chopped fresh sage

1 teaspoon chopped fresh rosemary

Grated rind ½ lemon and juice of 1 lemon

Sea salt

Freshly ground black pepper

1 glass dry red wine

This dish always reminds me romantically of natural, wild, gypsy life and brings back memories of cooking outside on hot summer days. A good roasted pepper salad with crostini *is the ideal accompaniment.*

METHOD

Cut the artichokes into 5 mm (¼ in) slices and simmer gently in plenty of salted water until just *al dente*. Refresh in very cold water. Mix together the marinade ingredients, and add the lamb and cooked artichokes. Marinate for at least 2–3 hours – the longer the better. Thread alternate pieces of lamb and artichoke onto 4 skewers, allowing 8 cubes of lamb for each skewer. Barbecue the skewers to taste.

Meanwhile, melt the butter in a pan, add the flour and cook gently, stirring, for 2 minutes. Gradually stir in the marinade ingredients and slowly bring to the boil. Simmer the sauce for 2–3 minutes and serve with the skewers.

OCA ARROSTO
Roast Goose

SERVES 10

4.5 kg (10 lb) fresh goose, oven-ready weight

2 tablespoons extra virgin olive oil

Sea salt

Freshly ground black pepper

150 ml (¼ pint) water

I know, I know: fat! We live in an age when fat is almost banned but, all the same, in my opinion the fact that a roasted goose produces a fifth of its weight in pure melted fat which you can use for producing other wonderful food is a bonus. The rest of the meat, when cooked properly, is a delicacy reminiscent of bygone times. I have included this recipe here in case you are lucky enough to get hold of a good goose and you want to know how to deal with it.

There are two cabbage dishes that are fantastic with goose Cavolo Rosso con Mele *and* Cavolo Cappuccio allo Speck *(see pages 162 and 178). You could also serve it with* Peperoni al Balsamico *(page 181). All these dishes taste even better eaten three days after cooking. (Remember to multiply the quantities of these recipes by 2½ to feed 10.)*

METHOD

Preheat the oven to 190°C/375°F/Gas 5.

Place the goose in a large roasting pan, breast up, and rub the oil into the skin. Season with salt and pepper inside and out. Pour the water into the pan, cover with foil, sealing round the edges, and roast the goose for 2 hours. Remove from the oven and baste with the juices from time to time to encourage a crisp skin. Return to the oven uncovered for a further 30 minutes.

Drain and reserve the fat, ensuring that you have none of the impurities. If necessary, chill the fat. The impurities will sink to the bottom and, after solidifying, the fat can be removed.

Rest the goose for 15 minutes. Remove the breast, carve and serve with the cabbage and pepper dishes as above.

BRACIOLETTE DI MAIALE AL VINO ROSSO
Pork Escalope with Red Wine

SERVES 4

1.5 kg (3 lb) pork fillet, cut into 12 x 5 mm (¼ in) slices

Sea salt

Freshly ground black pepper

20 g (¾ oz) freshly grated Parmesan

2 tablespoons finely chopped fresh flat-leaf parsley

1 tablespoon chopped fresh rosemary

12 fresh sage leaves

75 g (3 oz) butter

120 g (4½ oz) mortadella sausage, cut into 1 x 7.5 cm (½ x 3 in) sticks

8 baby gherkins (pickled in dill), cut in half

1 tablespoon extra virgin olive oil

1 red pepper, seeded

200 ml (7 fl oz) dry red wine

1 sprig fresh rosemary

25 g (1 oz) plain flour

In Italy, braciola *is an ambiguous word. In the South, it means a piece of meat on the bone while in other parts of Italy it is boned, rolled meat. To do this, you take a thinly cut piece of either pork escalope or fillet, beat it thin and then cut it to the right size so you can roll it up. If you do not have a wonderful* batticarne *(beater) then ask your butcher to do this for you.*

METHOD

Place each slice of pork fillet between 2 sheets of clingfilm and beat with a mallet until thin. Season with salt and pepper, sprinkle with Parmesan, parsley, rosemary and sage. Dot with 25 g (1 oz) of butter and place a stick of *mortadella* and half a gherkin on each. Roll up each escalope and secure with a cocktail stick.

Heat 25 g (1 oz) of the butter and the oil and brown the pork evenly and quickly over a moderate heat. Add half the pepper which you have finely diced and fry for 2 minutes. Stir in the wine and cook for 2 minutes to evaporate the alcohol. Reduce the heat and add the sprig of rosemary. Combine the remaining 25 g (1 oz) butter and flour in a small bowl and whisk into the sauce. Adjust the seasoning and transfer the *braciolette* to plates, removing the cocktail sticks and spooning over the sauce.

Serve with *Cipolline al Balsamico* (see page 165) and garnished with slices of the remaining half red pepper.

SCALOPPINE DI POLLO CON ERBE
Chicken Scaloppine with Herbs

SERVES 4

4 skinless chicken breasts, with the bone

2 tablespoons seasoned plain flour

75 g (3 oz) unsalted butter

1 tablespoon extra virgin olive oil

1 tablespoon each of the following finely chopped fresh herbs: chervil, dill, parsley, chives, basil, mint and rosemary

½ garlic clove, finely chopped

¼ fresh red chilli pepper, finely chopped, or to taste

Grated rind and juice of 1 lime

4 tablespoons chicken stock

4 tablespoons dry white wine

Sea salt

The combination of poached meat and herbs makes a very delicious dish for the summer which isn't too heavy, and may be enjoyed with Insalata di Fagiolini *(page 171). As in many other cases where pale meat is used, more fantasy is required in your use of herbs and flavouring to give a tasty result.*

If you cut the breast in strips from where it meets the bone in the shape of an octopus (see photograph, page 110–11) the greater surface area means more flavour can be absorbed – and the cooking time is reduced.

METHOD

Dust each chicken breast with the seasoned flour and fry over a moderate heat in half the butter and the oil to brown on both sides. Keep warm.

In the same pan, melt the remaining butter. Add the herbs, garlic, chilli and the rind and juice of the lime, stock and white wine. Return the chicken to the pan and poach for about 10 minutes until it is cooked. Season with salt and serve with the sauce.

Following pages (from left):

Coniglio San Domenico (page 123);

Scaloppine di Pollo con Erbe (above)

FARAONA CON PEVERADA
Guinea Fowl with Peverada Sauce

SERVES 4

1 x 1.5 kg (3 lb) guinea fowl

6 tablespoons olive oil

1 onion, finely chopped

1 carrot, finely chopped

400 g (14 oz) chicken livers (cleaned weight), finely chopped

100 g (4 oz) *speck*, cut into cubes

5 tablespoons chicken stock

4 tablespoons white wine

1 tablespoon white wine vinegar

Parsley, coarsely chopped

Salt and freshly ground black pepper

This dish is the gastronomic speciality of Treviso, a charming town not far from Venice. It is also famous for its radicchio, which the local restaurants serve cooked in hundreds of different ways, and sopressa, *a local type of salami.*

Guinea fowl is an elegant bird, which somehow tastes more like pork than chicken. This is an easy-to-prepare Sunday lunch which I make using speck *rather than* sopressa.

METHOD

Preheat the oven to 200°C, 400°F, Gas 6.

Singe the guinea fowl to ensure all the feathers are burned off and rub it with one tablespoon of the oil and salt. Place in a roasting tin and cook in the oven for about 1 hour.

Meanwhile, in a pan heat the remaining olive oil and sweat the onion over a low heat until transparent. Add the carrots, finely chopped chicken livers and speck. Fry gently for 10 minutes, then add the stock, wine and vinegar. Cook for a further 8 minutes. Remove from the heat, add the parsley and check the seasoning, adding salt and pepper to taste if necessary.

When the guinea fowl is cooked, remove it from the oven and serve with the sauce and *Cicoria in Umido* (page 176).

COSTOLETTA ALLA MILANESE
Veal Cutlets Milanese-style

SERVES 4

1 kg (2¼ lb) veal cutlets, each about 2.5 cm (1 in) thick

2 tablespoons seasoned plain flour

2 eggs, beaten

300 g (11 oz) fine dried breadcrumbs

90 g (3½ oz) unsalted butter

Lemon wedges, to serve

They say that when the Austrians reached Milan, they tasted the Costoletta alla Milanese *and adapted it for themselves as* Wienerschnitzel. *However,* Wienerschnitzel *in Vienna is made of pork rather than veal. This is one of the best ways to enjoy a rather delicate piece of meat, although purists would say that a real* Costoletta alla Milanese *is a cutlet complete with the bone.*

An ideal accompaniment would be a salad of pale, crisp Belgian chicory with a little rocket.

METHOD

Place the cutlets between 2 sheets of clingfilm and flatten them until they are 1 cm (½ in) thick. Dust with seasoned flour, patting off any excess, dip into beaten egg and coat in breadcrumbs.

Melt 20 g (¾ oz) of the butter in a large frying pan and fry the cutlets gently until golden brown on both sides, adding more butter if necessary. The cutlets are large so you will probably have to cook one or two at a time, keeping them warm in the oven until the last one is cooked.

Serve with wedges of lemon.

UCCELLETTI SCAPPATI CON POLENTA
'Flown-away' Sparrows with Polenta

SERVES 4

10 g (¼ oz) dried *porcini*
   mushrooms soaked in
   150 ml (¼ pint) lukewarm
   water

4 small chicken breasts sliced
   horizontally into 3 thin
   slices or 12 thin slices of
   turkey breast

Sea salt

Freshly ground black pepper

5 x 15 g (½ oz) slices *speck*

40 g (1½ oz) pine kernels

1 tablespoon finely chopped
   fresh flat-leaf parsley

10 g (¼ oz) butter

Seasoned plain flour

2 tablespoons extra virgin
   olive oil

Sparrow, originally called osei *in the Venetian dialect, were a speciality of that region, but this dish was also adopted by Bergamo. Here, the sparrows have 'flown away' to be replaced by rolls of chicken fillet!*

METHOD

Soak the dried *porcini* in the water for 30 minutes. Strain well, reserving the soaking liquor, and finely chop the mushrooms.

Put each slice of chicken or turkey between 2 sheets of clingfilm and beat with a mallet until thin. Season each slice with salt and pepper. Onto each *scaloppine* put one third of a slice of *speck*, a sprinkling of pine kernels, chopped *porcini*, a pinch of parsley and a few hazelnut-sized dots of butter. Roll up each *scaloppine* and secure with a cocktail stick and dust each with flour, patting off any excess. Brown gently in the heated oil, turning until they are cooked. Remove from the pan, remove the cocktail sticks and keep warm.

Add the shallot and garlic to the same pan and fry for 30 seconds before adding the fresh mushrooms. Fry gently for 3 minutes, stirring, then add the remaining slices of *speck*, cut into thin strips, and the red wine. Simmer for 2 minutes to evaporate the alcohol, then add 4 tablespoons of the *porcini* soaking liquor

FOR THE SAUCE

1 shallot, finely chopped

1 garlic clove, finely chopped

200 g (7 oz) fresh shiitake mushrooms

150 g (5 oz) fresh oyster mushrooms

2 tablespoons dry red wine

Sea salt

Freshly ground black pepper

1 teaspoon finely chopped fresh flat-leaf parsley

1 tablespoon *passata di pomodore* (sieved tomatoes)

FOR THE POLENTA

600 ml (1 pint) water

75 g (3 oz) instant polenta

50 g (2 oz) unsalted butter

2 tablespoons finely chopped fresh flat-leaf parsley

reserved earlier, salt and pepper, parsley and tomatoes. Cook for a further 2 minutes to develop the flavours then return the 'sparrows' to the pan. Simmer gently for 5 minutes, adding more soaking liquor if necessary. Season to taste.

In another pan, bring the water for the polenta to the boil. Add the polenta in a thin stream and stir until it has thickened. Add the butter and parsley, and serve with the 'false sparrows' and sauce.

FEGATO AL BALSAMICO
Liver with Balsamic Sauce

SERVES 4

1 large onion, finely sliced in
 rings

12 tablespoons extra virgin
 olive oil

8 x 75 g (3 oz) thin slices of
 calves' liver, cut into
 diagonal strips

Seasoned plain flour

4 tablespoons balsamic
 vinegar

Sea salt

Freshly ground black pepper

2 tablespoons chopped fresh
 chervil

In Italy you are given calves' liver when you are under the weather or a little anaemic, but it may be that its benefits are only an old wives' tale. However, liver is delicious especially when it is fried quickly so that it becomes crunchy on the outside and stays juicy on the inside.

To accompany this I would suggest small, cubed, sauté potatoes with garlic and rosemary.

METHOD

Fry the onion gently in the oil until it begins to brown. Meanwhile dust the liver with flour, patting off any excess, and put in to the pan increasing the heat and turning continuously for 2 minutes. Continue, adding the balsamic vinegar, salt and pepper, and serve sprinkled with chervil.

COSTOLINE DI AGNELLO RIPIENE
Stuffed Lamb Cutlets

SERVES 4

16 x 2.5 cm (1 in) lamb cutlets, French-trimmed

Sea salt

Freshly ground black pepper

75 g (3 oz) Fontina or Gruyère cheese, cut into slivers

16 large fresh sage leaves

75 g (3 oz) Parma ham, sliced

2 eggs, beaten with a pinch of sea salt

300 g (11 oz) fine dried breadcrumbs

Olive oil for shallow frying

This is a derivation of Cotoletta alla Valdostana *which uses local veal cutlets and Fontina cheese. The advantage of this recipe is that you can prepare it in advance and cook it at the last minute.*

'French-trimmed' cutlets can be prepared by your butcher. Most of the fat and other material is removed, leaving just the bone and the round lean meat section at the end.

METHOD

Cut down the centre of the meat of each cutlet until almost through and open out. Season with salt and pepper, then place a sliver of Fontina or Gruyère cheese on one side followed by a sage leaf and a little Parma ham. Fold over the other side of the meat. Dip the cutlets in egg and breadcrumbs to completely coat the meat. Press the cutlets together to seal and slightly flatten the meat. Shallow fry in moderately hot oil until golden on both sides.

Serve 4 cutlets per person with *Insalata di Fagiolini* (page 171) or with some *Cipolline al Balsamico* (page 165).

Following pages (from left): *Braciolette di Maiale al Vino Rosso* (page 108); *Costoline di Agnello Ripiene* (above)

MEDAGLIONI DI MANZO CON FUNGHI
Medallions of Beef with Mushrooms

SERVES 4

1 large onion, finely chopped

1 garlic clove, finely chopped

Chopped fresh red chilli pepper to taste

65 g (2½ oz) butter

1 tablespoon chopped fresh basil

2 tablespoons chopped fresh chives

1 tablespoon chopped fresh sage

400 g (14 oz) fresh hedgehog mushrooms, cleaned and sliced

Sea salt

120 ml (4 fl oz) beef stock, or a bouillon cube

2 tablespoons extra virgin olive oil

12 x 50 g (2 oz) medallions of beef, taken from the smaller end of the fillet

You can use both types of chanterelles, winter or summer, or fresh morels instead of the hedgehog mushrooms (whose Latin name is Hydnum repandum*). Always check a reliable reference book before picking wild mushrooms (see page 208).*

METHOD

Fry the onion, garlic and chilli gently in the butter until soft without colouring. Stir in the basil, chives and sage, cooking gently for 1 minute, then stir in the mushrooms and a little salt to extract the juices. When this happens, add the stock and fry for 1–2 minutes until the mushrooms are cooked but still *al dente*.

In another pan, heat the olive oil. When very hot, add the medallions of beef and brown quickly on both sides. Then the cooking time is up to you, depending on how well done you like your meat.

Transfer the medallions to warmed plates and spoon over the sauce. Serve with sautéd potatoes.

OSSOBUCO AL BAROLO
Shin of Veal with Barolo

SERVES 4

4 x 4 cm (½ in) thick slices of shin of veal, about 225 g (8 oz) each

Seasoned plain flour

6 tablespoons extra virgin olive oil

1 large onion, finely chopped

4 sticks celery, finely chopped

1 sprig fresh rosemary

4 tablespoons dry red wine, ideally Barolo

1 tablespoon vermouth

4 tablespoons beef stock, or a bouillon cube

Sea salt

Freshly ground black pepper

Osso *means bone,* buco *means hole, and this is exactly what this dish is. It is a piece of meat with a bone and a hole. The hole is full of wonderful stuff called marrow which becomes gelatinous when cooked and is very nourishing as well as delicious.*

This typical Milanese dish is usually served with saffron risotto. It makes an extremely satisfying winter meal.

METHOD

Preheat the oven to 150°C/300°F/Gas 2.

Dust the meat with flour, patting off any excess, and brown on both sides in hot oil. Add the onion, celery and rosemary to the pan and fry gently for 2 minutes. Add the red wine and vermouth and cook for 2 minutes to evaporate the alcohol. Add the beef stock, salt and pepper, cover and transfer to the oven. Braise for about 1 hour until tender. Serve with rice or, better still, saffron risotto.

BRACIOLE DI MAIALE DI ROSETTA
Rosetta's Loin of Pork

SERVES 4

4 x 275 g (10 oz) pork loin chops, including the bone

Seasoned plain flour for dusting

6 tablespoons extra virgin olive oil

400 g (14 oz) can plum tomatoes

1 garlic clove, finely chopped

1 bay leaf

1 fresh red chilli pepper, sliced, or to taste

100 ml (3½ fl oz) dry red wine

50 ml (2 fl oz) vinegar

50 ml (2 fl oz) water

½ teaspoon salt

Rosetta, a gamekeeper in the Sila, Calabria, gave me the idea for this way of cooking, which reduces effort in the kitchen and maximizes results. Because this sauce has a bite to it, it goes well with all fatty meats.

METHOD

Dust the pork with flour, patting off any excess. Brown in the oil for 5 minutes on both sides. Add the remaining ingredients, put on the lid and simmer very gently for about 1 hour until tender.

CONIGLIO SAN DOMENICO
San Domenico Rabbit

SERVES 4

1 kg (2¼ lb) rabbit, cleaned
weight

3 medium-sized globe artichokes

Juice of 1 lemon

6 tablespoons olive oil

1 large onion

100 g (4 oz) black Taggiasca
olives

6 leaves fresh sage

1 sprig marjoram

1 glass white wine

Chicken stock as required

1 teaspoon concentrated
tomato purée

2 teaspoons fresh parsley

Salt and freshly ground black
pepper

The four old Dominican monks I met at the fifteenth-century monastery of Taggia seem to have escaped the pressures of twentieth-century life. They grow everything they use in their back garden just as they did centuries ago and the artichokes, onions, salads, fruit and even their own raised rabbits looked so tempting that I had to cook this recipe for them. They enjoyed the feast very much and they invited me to return and spend some time with them. This recipe is dedicated to Padri Francesco Gusberti, Mario Raffaelo Icardi, Francesco Merlino and Attilio Pichino.

METHOD

Joint the cleaned rabbit and cut into medium-sized chunks. This can be done by your butcher.

Trim the artichokes up to the tender heart and cut into quarters. Put them in a bowl of water acidulated with the lemon juice to prevent discoloration.

Heat the oil in a large pan and fry the chopped onion. Then add the rabbit pieces, olives, sage, marjoram, salt and pepper, wine and some stock. Stir well, cover the pan with a lid and leave to simmer for 30 minutes, adding more stock if necessary. Add the artichokes, tomato purée and parsley and simmer for a further 10–15 minutes. Serve with *Patate Brasate al Forno* (see page 168).

ANITRA ALLA VERDI
Duck Verdi-style

SERVES 4

1.5 kg (3 lb) duck

2 medium-sized carrots

1 medium-sized onion

2 tablespoons olive oil

150 g (5 oz) Parma ham
   (mostly fat with little lean),
   minced to a paste

Sprig rosemary

I prepared this dish for the first time in Busseto near Parma, birthplace of the great maestro, Giuseppe Verdi, for the finalists in the vocal competition dedicated to him. The delicious simplicity of this dish would certainly meet the approval of one of the greatest composers of all time – at least I hope it would! It perfectly combines the local ingredients, duck and Parma ham.

METHOD

Preheat the oven to 220°C/425°F/Gas 7.

Singe the duck to ensure all the little feathers are burnt off, if necessary. Remove the giblets and season with salt and pepper.

Chop the onion and carrots into small cubes. Scatter into a roasting pan and place the duck on top. Rub the olive oil all over the duck. Take the minced Parma ham fat and spread over the top of the breast and place the sprig of rosemary on top. Cover with foil and place in the oven. After 1 hour remove the foil and roast for a further 15 minutes so that the duck becomes crispy.

If desired, you can serve the duck with the vegetables cooked with it. However, you should avoid the oil and fat left on the bottom of the pan. This is delicious with *Peperoni al Balsamico* (see page 181).

BRASATO AL NEBBIOLO
Braised Beef in Nebbiolo Wine

SERVES 4

2 medium-sized onions

2 carrots

3 sticks celery

1 kg (2¼ lb) beef topside

2 sprigs rosemary

100 g (4 oz) butter

5 tablespoons olive oil

5 sage leaves

2 garlic cloves

1 litre (1¾ pints) Nebbiolo
  wine

500 ml (18 fl oz) stock

Salt and freshly ground black
  pepper

The Nebbiolo grape is the father and mother of Barolo and is also used for making many other Piemontese wines, like Carema. Piemontese beef is particularly tasty. The union with Nebbiolo wine brings out the best in it and, after 2 hours cooking, it is tender and juicy. The alcohol evaporates during the cooking so you won't get tipsy when eating this robust but very tasty dish!

METHOD

Chop the onions, carrots and celery into small cubes and put to one side.

With a knife, slightly flatten the piece of meat to make it easier to roll. Place the rosemary inside, roll and bind with string. Season the joint all over with salt and pepper.

Heat the butter and oil in a large pan. Add the meat and seal very well until brown all over. Then add the chopped vegetables and fry until golden. Add the sage leaves and chopped garlic. When the vegetables have turned a nice colour, add the wine and the stock.

Cover with a lid and simmer for 1¾ hours. Take out and place on a serving dish with the sauce and vegetables.

Following pages (from left):

Luganiga al Vino Rosso (page 128);

Peperoni al Balsamico (page 181);

Anitra alla Verdi (page 124)

LUGANIGA AL VINO ROSSO
Luganiga Sausage in Red Wine

SERVES 4

675 g (1½ lb) luganiga
sausage

2 tablespoons olive oil

3 tablespoons red wine

2 sprigs rosemary

2 tablespoons stock

This, together with Pizzoccheri *(see page 68), is what I prepared for the fashion students of the Carlo Secoli Institute in Milan on the day of their end-of-year exams. It was a welcome break on a very tense day. They devoured everything within 10 minutes!*

Luganiga is an 'endless' pork sausage which you can buy by the metre in Italy. You can use 100% pork sausage, if you can get it, instead. In the winter, luganiga can be served cooked in a tomato sauce with polenta.

METHOD

Take the sausage and coil it tightly into a spiral. Fix some long cocktail sticks through the diameter of the sausage so that it is held solid and can be turned without breaking. Make the spiral as large as your frying pan.

Heat the oil in the frying pan and fry the sausage for 5 minutes on a high heat on one side. Then turn it over, lower the flame and cook for another 5 minutes. Add the wine, which will give a lovely flavour to the sausage, and place the rosemary sprigs in between the rings. Cook until the wine evaporates, about another 5–6 minutes, ensuring both sides are golden brown.

Remove the sausage and place on a preheated serving plate. Keep the pan on the heat, deglaze with the stock and pour this over the sausage.

Serve with *Bietole Brasate* (see page 177).

STINCO AL FORNO
Roast Shin of Veal

SERVES 10

4 kg (9 lb) shin of veal

2 garlic cloves, cut in quarters

5 sprigs rosemary

1 medium-sized onion

350 ml (12 fl oz) stock

4 tablespoons olive oil

Salt and freshly ground black pepper

In the Don Lisander Restaurant in Milan I enjoyed the speciality of the house, Stinco. An entire shin of veal was put in front of me from which a few succulent slices were carved off and this was served with lots of tender vegetables. It is a wonderful idea to cook this for a large party of at least 10 people, but make sure there are not many vegetarians among them! Serve with a mixture of vegetables such as courgettes, celeriac, carrots, leek and spinach.

METHOD

Preheat the oven to 180°C/350°F/Gas 4.

With a sharp knife, pierce the outer skin of the veal in several places and insert the rosemary and garlic pieces. Season the whole piece of meat with salt and pepper.

Slice the onion in rings and put in a roasting pan with the stock, oil and the meat. Cover with foil and roast in the oven for 1 hour 40 minutes. After 30 minutes, remove the foil. During cooking, baste the meat from time to time with the liquid. When it is cooked, keep the liquid, strain it and use as a sauce to serve with the meat.

FRITTO MISTO PIEMONTESE
Fried Meat Piemontese-style

SERVES 6

6 x 6 cm (2½ in) square flat
  pieces of the following
  meats: beef, lamb, pork,
  chicken, turkey, veal

6 small pork sausages

6 x 6 cm (2½ in) square
  pieces of pork liver, calves'
  liver, kidney, brain, or
  sweetbread

6 slices apple, peeled and
  cored

6 Amaretti biscuits

6 pieces sweet semolina
  (optional)

6 courgette flowers

6 aubergine slices

6 courgette slices

5 whole eggs, beaten

Salt

Dried breadcrumbs

Oil for frying

Lemon halves for serving

The work involved in making this dish is completely justified by the result for those who like food fried in breadcrumbs. A respectable fritto misto *has to have at least 13 different types of meat which are carefully prepared and shallow-fried at the last minute to arrive crispy and succulent on your plate. It is impossible to make this for many people, at the most it is for 4 or 6. This is without doubt the Piemontese speciality 'par excellence' and only enjoyable either in private or at a very good restaurant.*

You can choose any combination of ingredients, but take care to check the quantity of each. If you wish to use semolina, boil a thick paste with milk and a little sugar, stirring constantly. When cooled, pour onto a plate, allow to set and cut into small wedges.

METHOD

Once you are organized with all the ingredients at hand, near the stove, take a large frying pan and place on a moderate heat. First dip the pieces of meat, etc, in the egg mixture, to which you will have added salt to taste. Dust in breadcrumbs, shaking off any extra coating and fry gently in a little oil until golden on each side. Serve a mixture of your selection with lemon halves and a salad.

LENTICCHIE DI CASTELLUCCIO CON SALSICCE
Castelluccio Lentils with Sausage

SERVES 4

8 sausages, approximately 750 g (1½ lb), either pure pork or wild boar

400 g (14 oz) Castelluccio lentils

Leaves from 2 stalks of celery, chopped

2 garlic cloves

4 tablespoons virgin olive oil

1 fresh chilli, finely chopped

10 sun-dried tomatoes, halved

Salt

Stock, as required (a bouillon cube is fine)

Umbrian food is, in my opinion, one of the most authentic Italian cuisines and the least contaminated by modern catering methods. This recipe uses Castelluccio lentils which are full of iron and have a thin skin so they cook in a short time. You could, of course, use Puy lentils or green lentils instead.

Norcia pork sausages are made with locally raised animals and are the best I have ever tasted. Some people mix the pork with wild boar meat when in season and this adds a certain extra something.

METHOD

Boil the sausages in water for 30 minutes, then peel off the skins. Cover the lentils with water and then bring to the boil. Add the celery leaves and one whole clove of garlic and continue to cook until soft.

In another pan, heat the olive oil and fry the chilli, the other garlic clove, finely chopped, and the sun-dried tomatoes for one minute.

After removing and discarding the whole garlic clove, mix the lentil mixture with the tomatoes and chilli, and add the sausages. Allow to cook on a moderate heat for 10 minutes. The consistency must not be too soupy but neither must it be too thick so add stock if necessary. Add salt to taste and serve with bread.

CORATELLA DI AGNELLO
Ragout of Lamb Offal

SERVES 6

1 kg (2¼ lb) lamb's heart, liver and lungs

Virgin olive oil, for frying

2 medium onions, finely chopped

1 fresh chilli pepper, very finely chopped

1 sprig rosemary, bay leaves or sage (not together)

1 bottle dry white wine

Salt to taste

1 ripe tomato, seeded and cut into cubes (optional)

Because the Padrone (or boss) always used to get the better parts of an animal when it was slaughtered, the offal was usually discarded and given to the poor. Not today, however. Lamb's heart, liver and lungs are now a delicacy commanding very high prices. This speciality is also cooked, though slightly differently, in Southern Italy, but this is the Umbrian method. The original also includes the spleen and intestines, but for obvious reasons I suggest you use only the liver, heart and lungs.

Be brave, believe me, this is a very delicate and tasty dish.

METHOD

Clean the offal of any fat and unwanted pieces. Cut into very small slithers. Heat some oil in a pan and soften the onion with the chilli and whichever herb you are using. When golden, add the offal and stir from time to time. When the meat starts to brown, add some of the wine and tomato if desired. Cook, adding more wine as necessary, until soft and tender (about 30 minutes).

Serve with bread, rice, polenta or as a sauce for pasta.

PEARÀ
Bread and Pepper Sauce

SERVES 4

100 g (4 oz) bone marrow

100 g (4 oz) breadcrumbs

750 ml (1¼ pints) chicken stock

1 teaspoon freshly ground black pepper

Salt to taste

People say that Romeo was in love with this dish. Of course, the Veronesi would say that because this wonderful simple sauce is very typical of Verona.

This particular recipe comes from Giorgio Gioco, from the famous I Dodici Apostoli *restaurant in Verona. As he is the authority on Veronese food, this must be genuine. I made it again in my kitchen and could not stop eating it either by itself or with* cotechino, *a type of sausage made out of minced pork which, when cooked, remains juicy without being fatty. You can buy it pre-cooked from good Italian delicatessens.*

Ideally you should use breadcrumbs from Pugliese hard-dough bread, pasta di grano duro, *but you can use toasted ordinary breadcrumbs instead.*

METHOD

Preheat the oven to 240°C, 475°F, Gas Mark 9.

Place the whole bone in the oven for 20 minutes, and then carefully extract the marrow from the middle.

In a large pan, mix the bone marrow together with the breadcrumbs and stir over a moderate heat. Gradually mix in the stock, stirring all the time to avoid lumps. When all the liquid has been used up, add the pepper and some salt and mix thoroughly. Take off the heat and place in a bain-marie (a double boiler over a saucepan of simmering water) for 2 hours. The consistency should be silky and not too runny, rather like bread sauce.

Serve with boiled meat like chicken, *cotechino* or tongue.

SECOND
main courses – fish

I-PESCE

Most of Italy is surrounded by coastal waters and it also has many lakes and rivers in the North, so fish is not only easily and widely available, but also very much loved. For religious reasons, fish is eaten by almost everyone at least once a week, on Fridays. In addition, for dietary reasons, it is in great demand and therefore commands a very high price. Over-fishing of the sea – and a consequent scarcity of fish – plus pollution of the Mediterranean ensure that demand now outstrips supply, so fish needs to be imported from other parts of the world where it has been caught and frozen. Personally, I prefer freshly caught fish to frozen because, for me, frozen fish never seems to taste the same. I say this, even though I am very aware that many people argue that the freshness of so-called 'just caught' fish is sometimes questionable and that using frozen fish that has been caught and instantly shock-frozen on the boat – and kept like this until the defrosting process – has its advantages. As always in life, food is a matter of personal choice and taste.

Italians create the most amazing local specialities in whatever form they eat fish, from anchovies to tuna in oil, from salted and air-dried mullet roe to *mosciame* (air-dried tuna fillet) to *stoccafisso* (air-dried cod) or *baccalà* (salt cod), even herring. Take, for example, the shocking Sicilian combination of orange and salted herring salad! A delicate *Fritto Misto di Pesce* (mixed fried fish) from Liguria however is an absolutely delightful dish, as is the fillet of *lavarelli* (bream) freshly caught on Lake Maggiore.

In the mountains far away from the coast where, for obvious reasons, the fish cannot arrive as quickly and freshly as in coastal areas, there are many recipes for *baccalà* and *stoccafisso*. The desire in these remote regions not to miss out

Previous pages: *Trota in Cartoccio* (page 150)

on the joy provided by fish dishes is celebrated in the *Sagra dello Stoccafisso*, an annual fish festival that takes over the entire village of Badalucco in Liguria. Olga Panizzi, known as the 'Queen of Stoccafisso', has become famous for making a wonderful dish using salted fish, plus local olive oil and dried wild *porcini*. This is even more surprising when you consider that the stockfish comes from Norway!

The unique variety of the 'catches' in the Adriatic from Grado to Chioggia, south of Venice, makes this *the* place to enjoy rare fish specialities. Cuttlefish roe, for example, when boiled and dressed with lemon juice is a delicacy without comparison. If you want to taste such things at their very best, go, like the Venetians themselves, to *La Madonna* near the Rialto bridge. I would certainly love to have daily deliveries of such ingredients to my London restaurant, but I have to make do with bigger fish from northern waters.

BRANZINO ALLE ERBE
Sea Bass with Herbs

SERVES 4

1 x 1.75 kg (4 lb) sea bass,
cleaned, scaled and fins
removed

1 lemon, cut into 7 slices

2 sprigs fresh thyme

6 tablespoons extra virgin
olive oil

1 tablespoon finely chopped
fresh mint

2 stalks fresh flat-leaf
parsley, finely chopped

1 tablespoon finely chopped
fresh fennel leaves
(optional)

20 leaves fresh basil, finely
chopped

1 bunch fresh chives, finely
chopped

1 tablespoon celery leaves,
finely chopped

Juice ½ lemon

Sea salt

Freshly ground black pepper

The Italians prefer sea bass to any other fish. They call it spigola *or* branzino. *It is one of the most beautiful fish, with white, firm meat which keeps a fantastic taste of the sea. Here, it is cooked in foil and when you open the parcel a wonderful aroma is released.*

Serve it with freshly boiled new potatoes and green beans sautéed in a little butter. Remember to collect the juices and herbs and spoon them over each serving.

When you buy a spigola *make sure that it is very fresh, with clear eyes, very red gills and your fishmonger's guarantee that it is really fresh. Under no circumstances should you cook this dish with a frozen fish. However, feel free to choose your own preferred fish (such as grey mullet) should you not find sea bass.*

METHOD

Preheat the oven to 200°C/400°F/Gas 6.

Dry the sea bass thoroughly with kitchen paper. Take a large piece of foil and place it in an ovenproof dish. Put the lemon slices onto it and place the fish on top. Season the inside of the fish, adding the sprigs of thyme. Using your hands, massage 4 tablespoons of the oil into the skin of the fish and season with salt and pepper.

Mix the mint, parsley, fennel leaves, basil, chives and celery leaves. Place half the herbs inside the fish. Bring up the sides of the foil to enclose the fish and seal the edges carefully – you will need to open and seal the foil again at a later stage. Bake for 30 minutes.

Remove from the oven and carefully open the foil. Mix the remaining herbs with the lemon juice and remaining 2 tablespoons of oil and spoon over the top of the fish. Leave the foil open but gathered round the fish to protect it from the fierce heat of the oven and bake for a further 5 minutes. Make sure the fish is cooked by piercing the flesh by the backbone.

To serve the fish, make an incision along its back, detach the fillet from the head and tail and remove completely from the fish. Cut each fillet in two. Turn over and repeat. Spoon over the herbs and juices and serve.

ROMBO CON CHIODINI E ORECCHIE DI JUDA
Turbot with Honey Fungus and Judas Ears

SERVES 4

5 g (⅛ oz) dried *porcini* mushrooms, soaked for 30 minutes in 150 ml (¼ pint) tepid water

100 g (4 oz) honey fungus

4 tablespoons extra virgin olive oil

200 g (7 oz) Judas Ear mushrooms

1 garlic clove, crushed

1 tablespoon finely chopped fresh flat-leaf parsley

Sea salt

Freshly ground black pepper

4 x 175 g (6 oz) fillets of turbot

I put this recipe on the menu of my restaurant years ago and it is still one of the favourites. Of course, you have to have the best and freshest of ingredients. You can also make this with other funghi, *such as horn of plenty and bay boletus, and the result is still spectacular. If these too are unavailable, use cultivated shiitake and oyster mushrooms. If you do collect your own mushrooms, check a reference book first (see page 208).*

You can find Judas Ears in Chinese shops where they are also called black or Wood Ear fungus and you can reconstitute them in water. Take care when you fry the Judas Ears because they can explode in fat.

If you can't get turbot, use halibut or monkfish instead.

METHOD

Soak the dried mushrooms in tepid water for 30 minutes and squeeze dry, reserving the soaking liquor. If the honey fungus is fresh, boil it in salted water for 10 minutes before sautéing in half the oil.

Fry the Judas Ears gently in the remaining oil with the garlic until they start to crackle in the pan. Remove from the heat and stir in the parsley and honey fungus. Squeeze the *porcini* dry, chop and add them to the pan along with the soaking liquor. Season to taste with salt and pepper.

Meanwhile, in a separate pan, seal the fish fillets on both sides in hot olive oil. Tip in the contents of the other pan. Fry for 2 more minutes and serve.

INSALATA DI BACCALÀ
Salt Cod Salad

SERVES 4

450 g (1 lb) salt cod

Juice 1 lemon

1 garlic clove, cut in thick slices

2 tablespoons finely chopped fresh flat-leaf parsley

4 tablespoons extra virgin olive oil

8 black olives, stoned

1 tablespoon capers

Freshly ground black pepper or cayenne pepper to taste

Salt cod, the poor man's fish, is still cheap compared to some of the more exotic fresh fish. It is extremely versatile and generally used in every Italian region, cooked in hundreds of ways. It can be bought in Italy already soaked to save time. You will find it in good delicatessens.

METHOD

Cut the salt cod into chunks and cover it, skin-down, with water for 24 hours, changing the water every 6 hours. Put in a pan, cover with fresh water and bring to the boil, gently simmering for 1 hour or until the cod is cooked. Drain and when cool discard the bones and the skin and break with your hands into flakes. Put in a serving dish and mix carefully with the lemon juice, garlic, parsley, oil, olives and capers. No salt is needed because the cod will have kept part of its own salt despite the soaking and cooling. A couple of twists of freshly ground black pepper will do the trick, though I prefer a little cayenne pepper.

CALAMARI RIPIENI CON RISOTTO AL PESTO
Stuffed Squid with Pesto Risotto

SERVES 4

165 g (5½ oz) fresh white bread

150 ml (¼ pint) milk

1 egg

165 g (5½ oz) spinach, cooked, squeezed weight

1 tablespoon chopped fresh dill

1 tablespoon pine kernels

Rind ½ lemon

1 tablespoon freshly grated Parmesan

20 baby squid, about 500 g (1 lb 4 oz), cleaned weight

1 small garlic clove, very finely chopped

½ fresh red chilli pepper, chopped, or to taste

Squid is a classic flavour of the Mediterranean but is available worldwide. For this recipe, use the smaller variety.

You will need to prepare the squid for cooking by detaching the body from the tentacles and pulling out the insides from the body. Peel off the purple skin and the fins and discard. Cut the tentacles from the squids' heads and squeeze out the beak from the middle.

It is the body that will be used as a container for the stuffing. There are many fillings you can use, but I have discovered that the best thing is to incorporate the chopped sautéed tentacles with the other ingredients. This dish can be eaten either hot or cold.

METHOD

Preheat the oven to 240°C/475°F/Gas 9.

Soak the bread in the milk, squeeze dry and mix the bread pulp with the egg. Add the spinach, dill, pine kernels, lemon rind and Parmesan.

Prepare the squid as described in the introduction. Coarsely chop the tentacles. Fry the garlic and chilli in 1 tablespoon of the oil for 30 seconds. Add the tentacles and cook over a high heat for 1 minute. Cool a little and add to the stuffing. Mix well. Season to taste with salt.

Previous pages (from left): *Rombo con Chiodini e Orecchie di Juda* (page 140); *Fritto Misto di Burano* (page 146)

5 tablespoons olive oil

Juice ½ lemon

Juice 2 oranges

Sea salt

1 small onion, finely chopped

2 tablespoons olive oil

200 g (7 oz) risotto rice
  (arborio, vialone nano or
  carnaroli)

750 ml (1¼ pint) chicken stock

2 tablespoons pesto sauce
  (page 54)

Using a piping bag, half fill the cavities of the squid with the stuffing and secure the ends with a cocktail stick. The stuffing will swell during cooking.

Heat 4 tablespoons of oil in a flameproof dish and fry the squid for about 5 minutes on both sides. Add the lemon and orange juice and transfer to the oven. Bake for 10 minutes.

Meanwhile, to prepare the risotto, fry the onion in the oil until soft, add the rice and fry for a minute, coating each grain well in oil. Add the stock, which you are keeping hot, a ladle at a time until it has all been absorbed and you have a creamy consistency. Stir in the pesto sauce and set to one side.

Allow 5 pieces of squid for each person and serve each portion with a little of the sauce and some risotto.

FRITTO MISTO DI BURANO
Mixed Fried Fish Burano-style

SERVES 4

400 g (14 oz) fresh eel, cleaned weight, cut into chunks

8 giant Mediterranean prawns, body peeled but head and tail still attached

150 g (5 oz) squid or cuttle-fish, cleaned weight, including tentacles

Plain flour as required for dusting

Olive oil for deep frying

Salt

2 lemons

On the small and very pretty island of Burano near Venice, once Italy's centre of handmade embroidery, the gondola regatta is quite a prestigious event. The entire village (about 800 people) takes part. While the youngsters row in the race, the others prepare the most delicious Fritto Misto di Pesce *which is sold to the thousands of people who travel from all over the area. Every coastal region in Italy has its own* Fritto Misto di Pesce, *but only a few have a* laguna *from which they can catch such delicious fish.*

METHOD

Preheat a deep fryer to 190°C, 375°F.

Sprinkle all the fish with salt and coat each piece in flour, ensuring each whole piece of fish is covered. Shake off excess flour. Deep fry the fish for 2–3 minutes, starting with the eel, then the squid or cuttlefish, and fry for an additional 2 minutes. Lastly add the prawns and fry for a minute or two. All the pieces of fish should be a golden-brown colour when cooked. Drain on absorbent paper, then serve with lemon halves on preheated plates.

In Burano, they serve this on pieces of old-fashioned butcher's paper, which I find rather amusing.

Burano's gondola regatta

FRUTTI DI MARE GRATINATI
Baked Shellfish

SERVES 4

8 small queen scallops

4 oysters (optional)

24 large mussels

8 razor shells

8 clams

8 tablespoons extra virgin olive oil

1 garlic clove first crushed, then very finely chopped

4 tablespoons dried fine breadcrumbs

2 tablespoons finely chopped fresh flat-leaf parsley

Sea salt

Freshly ground black pepper

Lemon wedges

Frutti di mare *are fully appreciated in the Mediterranean because they can be eaten fresh from the sea and raw with the help of a little lemon juice. Every seaside resort in Italy has its own speciality based on* frutti di mare *either raw, baked or grilled.*

One of the most delightful ways to eat shellfish is as described below, just sprinkled with good olive oil, parsley, garlic, breadcrumbs and a little salt. You can use all sorts of shellfish for this.

METHOD

Preheat the oven to 240°C/475°F/Gas 9.

First prepare the shellfish. Detach the scallops and oysters carefully from their shells and separate the coral from the white flesh of the scallop. Put the mussels, razor shells and clams in a pan, cover and place over a high heat for 1–2 minutes until the shells open. Remove the top shell of each mussel, discarding any that do not open. Mix the oil and chopped garlic.

Arrange each shell, with its own meat inside, on an ovenproof dish. Sprinkle with breadcrumbs, parsley, salt and pepper and sprinkle the garlic and oil on top. Bake for 10–15 minutes until brown. Serve hot, garnished with lemon wedges, but they are also delicious cold.

BRODETTO DI PESCE
Fish Broth

SERVES 4

36 large mussels, tightly closed

8 raw king prawns

200 g (7 oz) monkfish

8 tablespoons extra virgin olive oil

½ garlic clove, crushed

¼ fresh red chilli pepper, chopped, or to taste

100 g (4 oz) fennel or fennel tops

1 large tomato, coarsely chopped

750 ml (1¼ pints) fish stock

Rind 1 lemon

8 anchovy fillets

Sea salt

Freshly ground black pepper

Brodetto *is the diminutive of* brodo *and means literally 'small broth'. Although it is usually made with meat or chicken here I use fish stock. You can buy this from good supermarkets or easily make it at home by asking the fishmonger for tasty bits and pieces. The fishmonger will also be able to help you with the choice of fish because it will all depend on the catch of the day.*

This is wonderful eaten with the croûtons of garlic bread called fettunta. *Make these by toasting slices of bread and gently rubbing a garlic clove over them, and then brush with a little extra virgin olive oil.*

METHOD

Scrub the mussels under cold running water and, with a small sharp knife, scrape away the beard. Wash in several changes of cold water until the water is left clean. Peel the prawns. Remove all membrane from the monkfish and cut into 5 cm (2 in) pieces.

Heat the oil and fry the garlic and chilli for 15 seconds only. Add the fennel and tomato and cook for 2 minutes, then add the stock, lemon rind and the fish and shellfish. Simmer for 10 minutes until all the shellfish are open and cooked. Check the seasoning and serve.

TROTA IN CARTOCCIO
Trout in a bag

SERVES 4

4 x 300 g (11 oz) trout

200 g (7 oz) fennel

1 large lemon

4 sprigs parsley

65 g (2½ oz) butter

**Salt and feshly ground black
   pepper**

Enveloping a fish in a leaf, clay or salt is a method that was used by the ancient Romans. This form of cooking retains the juices in the envelope, enabling the food to be gently cooked in hot moisture and filling it with flavour.

You may use either greaseproof paper or aluminium foil, taking care not to envelope the fish too tightly or it will come into contact with the paper which would remove the skin when you open the parcel. The best effect is achieved when the parcel is opened in front of the guests so they can inhale the wonderful aroma. Branzino alle Erbe *(see page 138) is cooked in a similar way.*

METHOD

Preheat the oven to 200°C/400°F/Gas 6.

Clean, gut and scale the trout or ask the fishmonger to do it. Chop the fennel and slice the lemon very finely.

Scatter the chopped fennel and a few lemon slices in the middle of 4 sheets of greaseproof paper. Season the fish with salt and pepper and place on the fennel. Place a couple of lemon slices inside the fish with a sprig of parsley. Place the remaining lemon slices over the fish and dot with butter.

Seal the edges of the paper making a parcel, place on a baking tray and cook for 20 minutes.

Serve on a long plate opening the parcels in front of your guests.

LAVARELLI IN TEGLIA
Baked Fillets of Lake Bream

SERVES 4

4 x 300 g (11 oz) fillets lake bream

Plain white flour for dusting

120 g (4½ oz) butter

8 sage leaves

Salt and freshly ground black pepper

This is a delicate and tasty way of cooking lake or river fish. Lavarelli and coregoni are fished regularly on Lake Maggiore and this is one of the best ways to eat them. In a similar way you can use fillets of other fish with wonderful results.

METHOD

Preheat the oven to 200°C/400°F/Gas 6.

Dust each fillet in flour and lay on a baking dish adding salt and pepper. Meanwhile, put the butter and sage leaves in a pan and fry until foamy. Pour over the fillets of fish and bake in the oven for 7 minutes.

ZUPPA DI PESCE DI SAN GIOVANNI
Fish Soup

SERVES 6

2 green fennel tops

2.5 litres (4½ pints) water

6 tablespoons olive oil

1 small onion, finely chopped

1 small red chilli

4 tablespoons tomato pulp

350 g (12 oz) monkfish, cut into 2.5 cm (1 in) chunks

350 g (12 oz) John Dory, cleaned, filleted and cut into 2.5 cm (1 in) chunks

300 g (11 oz) red mullet, cleaned, filleted and cut into 2.5 cm (1 in) chunks

100 g (4 oz) octopus, cut into 2.5 cm (1 in) slices, tentacles removed

100 g (4 oz) squid, cut into 2.5 cm (1 in) rings

100 g (4 oz) cuttlefish, cut into 2.5 cm (1 in) strips

12 clams

12 mussels

100 g (4 oz) large prawns, shelled

6 scallops, shelled

2 tablespoons fresh parsley, coarsely chopped

Salt and freshly ground black pepper, to taste

The San Giovanni *restaurant in Casarza is where I came across this Ligurian speciality. The fairy queen of that kitchen, Pinuccia, is an ex-fishmonger and knows the importance of freshness to a good fish soup. This soup is known locally as* cacciucco. *You need to use good tasty fish for this dish.*

METHOD

To make the fish stock, take the fish heads and bones and place in a large pan with the fennel and the water. Bring to the boil and simmer for 30 minutes.

Heat the oil in a large pan, add the onion and chilli and fry for a couple of minutes. Stir in the tomato pulp. Add the chunks of monkfish, John Dory, red mullet, octopus, squid and cuttlefish to the pan and a litre (1¾ pints) of the fish stock and leave to simmer for 10 minutes. Then add the clams, mussels, prawns and scallops and cook for a further 5–6 minutes. Add the parsley and season with salt and pepper.

When dividing the soup, ensure that it is done equally and fairly so that everyone gets a bit of everything!

Please note that if you prefer a thicker consistency, add a very thinly sliced potato during cooking.

TRIGLIE INCAZZATE
Angry Red Mullet

SERVES 4

75 g (3 oz) butter

1 tablespoon sage, finely
chopped

1 tablespoon rosemary, finely
chopped

1 tablespoon parsley, finely
chopped

1 tablespoon fresh chilli
pepper, coarsely chopped

4 red mullet, 250 g (9 oz)
each, scaled and filleted

1 glass red wine

Salt

Sprig of rosemary, to
decorate

'Incazzate', *like 'arrabbiate', means literally 'angry' but in cookery has come to mean hot due to the addition of chilli.*

At the end of a long, hard photo shoot for this book which had lasted several days, we suddenly realized that one of the dishes was a little unphotogenic and I had only a few angry minutes to create another. The idea for this recipe came out of the heat of that moment, but don't be put off!

METHOD

Heat the butter in a pan, add the herbs and chilli and stir-fry for half a minute. Add the fillets of fish and fry for 1–2 minutes on each side. Set aside the fish and deglaze the pan with the wine. Taste for salt. Reunite the fish with the sauce, warm and serve decorated with a sprig of rosemary.

Following pages (from left): *Triglie Incazzate* (above); *Zuppa di Pesce di San Giovanni* (page 152)

STOCCAFISSO BADALUCCHESE
Stockfish Badalucco-style

SERVES 6

1 whole stockfish, cut into chunks (use a saw if necessary)

4 tablespoons olive oil

10 anchovy fillets

20 g (¾ oz) pine kernels

4 garlic cloves

20 g (¾ oz) dried *porcini*, soaked in water

Sprig fresh marjoram

2 tablespoons concentrated tomato purée

300 ml (½ pint) chicken stock

2 tablespoons parsley

Each year the village of Badalucco in the Ligurian hills near Taggia, not far from San Remo, celebrates the Stockfish Festival. Most of the stoccafisso (dried cod) is produced in the Lofoten Islands, Norway, and every year they send 500 kg as a present to the Badalucchesi.

The word comes from the German Stock Fisch, 'fish as hard as a stick', and this is literally true of this preserved cod. It used to be for poor people who could not afford fresh fish. Only the inventiveness of poor people has enabled it to become a very desirable dish for everyone and nowadays, it is regarded as a delicacy.

Begin the preparations for this dish 4 days in advance.

METHOD

Soak the fish in water for 4 days, changing the water daily. After the 4-day soaking, boil the fish in clean water for 3–4 hours.

Meanwhile put the oil in a large pan and very gently fry the anchovies, pine kernels, garlic, *porcini* (with its juice), marjoram and the tomato purée. Cook for an hour on a very low heat so that it bubbles gently and produces a thick, tasty sauce. Drain the fish, remove the bones. Pile the bones on the bottom of a large pan and alternate layers of fish flesh and sauce. The bones give extra flavour. Cook this for 40 minutes, adding the stock. Serve sprinkled with parsley. You can accompany this with polenta, boiled potatoes or bread and wash it down with plenty of red wine!

CODA DI ROSPO
ALLA CONTE CARLO
Monkfish Conte Carlo

SERVES 6

1.5 kg (3 lb) waxy potatoes, peeled and very thinly sliced

20 sage leaves

Abundant extra virgin olive oil

1.5 kg (3 lb) monkfish, cut into flat fillets

100 g (4 oz) freshly grated Parmesan

Salt and freshly ground pepper to taste

A cooking Count is not the kind of person you meet every day. Conte Carlo Maria Rocca from Venice is one of the most charming gourmet cooks I have ever encountered. It was delightful to shop with him at the Rialto market where he was well known and where he showed great talent in spotting the best ingredients.

After an ombra, *a glass of wine, in* Bacchero, *a typical Venetian wine bar, I sampled real Venetian food. The Count is a great entertainer and he created this simple and delicious dish. Monkfish can be replaced with John Dory, turbot or halibut, so long as the fish is boneless. You need to slice the potatoes to about 1 mm thick, so use a mandolin or food processor for best results.*

METHOD

Preheat the oven to 200°C, 400°F, Gas Mark 6.

Arrange half the thinly sliced potatoes in a thin layer in a large ovenproof dish with half the sage. Sprinkle with some oil, cover with the fillets and sprinkle with half of the Parmesan. Cover with another layer of potato slices, sprinkle with some more oil, add the rest of the sage leaves and the remaining Parmesan, salt and pepper. Bake in the oven for about 1 hour until the potatoes are tender.

VEGETALI
vegetables and

E CONTORNI
accompaniments

It is a real joy to communicate the passion I feel for Italian food, but especially the way Italians produce and use the most wonderful array of vegetables. When I am in an Italian street market, I visit *all* the stalls to locate the best offers. I would never buy everything from one stall if the quality wasn't the highest available. This shopping around is essential if you want to go home with the best ingredients for a wonderful meal; the other essential, of course, is knowing what to do with what you have bought!

Many people can recognize good-quality vegetables at a glance, but do not know how to make the best use of them. When tender artichokes are in season, it's worth buying them to stuff, even if this involves a little more preparation. Likewise, with multi-coloured freshly picked borlotti beans: pod and boil them and what a wonderful salad you can make!

In Italy, it is common for market-traders and greengrocers to do the initial cleaning and sorting of the vegetables for you. This saves you preparation time, but you will probably have to pay a little extra for the produce. You can, for example, find cleaned artichoke hearts, prepared mixed vegetables for minestrone and cleaned salad mixture, including wild *rucola* (rocket), fennel or chervil.

All the instinctive, special, loving, marketing measures of market traders and greengrocers can never quite be matched by supermarkets. That is another reason why it is such a pleasure to buy in street markets. One can also often receive very good, useful and inspiring tips about how to cook certain items. Many cooks or young housewives have received stimulating cookery lessons in this way. To me it is horrific that this is dying away, being replaced by

Previous pages: *Peperoni al Balsamico* (page 181)

distributors who buy cheap produce in foreign countries using shelf-life as their criterion rather than taste or quality.

Regional individuality is what makes Italian food so desirably different. For example, it is interesting to note how people emigrating from the South to the more prosperous North took with them their own eating traditions, specialities and produce. So, during the last thirty or so years, the more prosperous population of the northern regions have been able to buy many previously unknown vegetables and fruit. Now the Milanese or Torinese quite naturally buy Sicilian, Pugliese or Calabrian produce freshly cut or picked and sent through the night to local northern markets.

This movement of merchandise has not detracted from quality because the produce usually comes from natural environments that produce the best taste and flavour. The same cannot be said, however, for local produce that is raised in greenhouses and picked unripe to allow for easier transport and storage. Such practices certainly take their toll on taste. In Italy today, as in so many other places, the first signs of agricultural industrialization are gradually appearing. I can only hope that this will not have too great an impact on and kill off the small producers who deliver the best traditional goods.

The many different ways in which vegetables can be served is one good reason why you should not miss the main courses on the menu. Being a vegetarian in Italy is a great pleasure indeed!

CAVOLO ROSSO CON MELE
Red Cabbage with Apples

SERVES 4

1 small onion, finely chopped

3 whole dried cloves

2 tablespoons extra virgin
olive oil

500 g (1 lb 4 oz) red cabbage,
finely shredded

350 g (12 oz) Bramley apples,
peeled, cored and thinly
sliced

375 ml (13 fl oz) chicken
stock, or a bouillon cube

10 g (¼ oz) caster sugar

Pinch ground cinnamon

Sea salt

Freshly ground black pepper

2 teaspoons white wine
vinegar

Red cabbage, being spicy, goes well with all sorts of game, especially poultry such as goose and duck. I sometimes add some sweet apple juice instead of sugar, with wonderful results. I usually make more than necessary because it is so very good to eat and looks like a jam a couple of days later.

METHOD

Fry the onion and cloves gently in the oil until soft but without colouring. Add the cabbage, apples, stock, sugar, cinnamon, salt and pepper. Simmer over a moderate heat for about 35 minutes until the apples have dissolved and the cabbage is tender, stirring from time to time to prevent sticking, and adding more water if necessary. Add the vinegar and simmer for a further 5 minutes.

FUNGHI TRIFOLATI
Truffled Mushrooms

SERVES 4

500 g (1¼ lb) fresh wild mushrooms, or cultivated button mushrooms

1 garlic clove, very finely chopped

6 tablespoons extra virgin olive oil

Salt and pepper to taste

2 tablespoons finely chopped parsley

Trifolare is a way of cooking in Italy which involves sautéing with the addition of parsley. You may 'trifolare' courgettes, aubergines or as in this case, funghi, *wild or cultivated. The word comes from* trifola *(truffle in the Piemontese dialect) and probably when truffles were not as sought-after and expensive as they are today, they were cooked this way. This is a dish that can be eaten by itself, accompanied by bread or served as a side dish to meat or fish. If you are intending to pick your own wild mushrooms, it is essential to consult a reliable reference book first (see page 208).*

METHOD

Clean the mushrooms well, discarding all the impurities – try not to wash if possible. Heat the oil in a pan until very hot, but not smoky. Add all the mushrooms and sauté or stir-fry for 10 minutes, until you see the mushrooms reduce in volume. Then add the garlic and sauté for another 10 minutes. Add salt, pepper and parsley and serve.

FAVE ALLO SPECK
Broad Beans with Speck

SERVES 4

2 garlic cloves

4 tablespoons extra virgin olive oil

50 g (2 oz) *speck*, cut into strips

1 kg (2¼ lb) fresh, young broad beans

Salt and pepper to taste

Speck *is a smoked ham speciality left in Northern Italy by the Austrian invasion and it is used especially widely in the South Tyrol, where the Austrian influence is still very strong. The popularity of this shoulder ham has nevertheless spread in recent years to the rest of Italy where it is used as an alternative to the milder Parma ham. I like to use* speck *to impart its special smoky flavour to many dishes.*

METHOD

Fry the garlic in the oil very briefly. Add the *speck* and broad beans and a little water, just to cover the beans. Put the lid on and cook on a moderate heat for 15 minutes. Add salt and pepper and finish cooking without the lid to let the water evaporate.

CIPOLLINE AL BALSAMICO
Baby Onions with Balsamic Sauce

SERVES 4

225 g (8 oz) baby onions, peeled

3 tablespoons extra virgin olive oil

1 tablespoon balsamic vinegar

2 tablespoons red wine

Sea salt

These cipolline *with their sweet and sour taste are delicious and can be served as part of an* antipasto *or to accompany hot and cold meat dishes.*

METHOD

Blanch the onions in plenty of boiling salted water for 15 minutes. Drain well. Sauté gently in the olive oil until golden brown. Add the vinegar, red wine and salt to taste, and cook briefly to allow the alcohol to evaporate.

Following pages (from left):

Fave allo Speck (page 164);

Pomodori Ripieni (page 173)

PATATE BRASATE AL FORNO
Braised Baked Potatoes

SERVES 4

1 large onion, coarsely chopped

750 g (1¾ lb) waxy potatoes, peeled and cut into 5mm (¼ in) slices

½ tablespoon each chopped fresh basil, sage, chives and parsley

250 g (9 oz) ripe tomatoes, coarsely chopped

Sea salt

Freshly ground black pepper

3 tablespoons extra virgin olive oil

This is a peasant meal made in the country when everyone is busy and no one has time to cook! It is just thrown into the oven without a lot of care, but funnily enough it is this that gives the perfect taste to the dish. You can eat it by itself or serve it with any roasted meat.

METHOD

Preheat the oven to 240°C/475°F/Gas 9.

Put all the ingredients into a roasting pan and mix together with your hands. Bake for about 1 hour until the potatoes are cooked.

INSALATA DI PEPERONI ARROSTO
Roast Pepper Salad

SERVES 4

2 red peppers

2 yellow peppers

1 garlic clove or 1 teaspoon garlic oil

Sea salt

1 tablespoon coarsely chopped fresh flat-leaf parsley

4 tablespoons extra virgin olive oil

I do not know anybody who does not like peppers prepared this way. Even my wife, who finds peppers usually give her indigestion, loves this dish. They can accompany any meat or fish but I think of them as one of the most fantastic things you can find in the fridge when you come home late in need of a snack! Dip a piece of bread into the oil and crown it with a roasted pepper. It is the most delightful morsel on your way to bed. It is also one of the most versatile accompaniments to all kinds of main dishes.

METHOD

Blacken the peppers, preferably over a charcoal grill or otherwise in a very hot oven. When cool, remove the skin and seeds, retaining any juices, and slice the peppers into 2.5 cm (1 in) strips. To the peppers and their juices add the garlic (sliced coarsely so it will be visible and you can avoid eating it!) or garlic oil, salt, parsley and olive oil and mix well. Leave for a few hours to allow the flavours to develop.

FINOCCHIO GRATINATO
Baked Fennel

SERVES 4

3 fennel bulbs, about 500 g
  (1 lb 2 oz)
Sea salt
Freshly ground black pepper
A pinch of freshly grated
  nutmeg
40 g (1½ oz) unsalted butter
1 garlic clove, crushed
2 tablespoons freshly grated
  Parmesan

In Italy, fennel is sometimes eaten as a fruit instead of dessert, using the tender central part. However, here is a delicious way of cooking it which you can serve with all sorts of dishes, both meat and fish. I suggest you have this accompanying Fritto Misto di Burano *(page 146).*

METHOD

Preheat the oven to 240°C/475°F/Gas 9.

To prepare the fennel, remove the stalks and tough outer leaves. Cut each head in half and then quarter each half. Simmer the fennel in plenty of salted water until *al dente*. Drain very well and place in an ovenproof gratin dish. Sprinkle with salt, pepper and nutmeg. Melt the butter, add the garlic and infuse for 1–2 minutes, then pour over the fennel. Sprinkle with Parmesan and bake for 15 minutes until sizzling.

INSALATA DI FAGIOLINI
Green Bean Salad

SERVES 4

600 g (1 lb 6 oz) French beans, topped and tailed

2 sprigs fresh mint

2 thick slices garlic clove

5 tablespoons extra virgin olive oil

Sea salt

Juice 1 lemon (optional) or a few drops of wine vinegar

This is one of my favourite vegetable dishes, not just because it takes very little time to prepare, but also because the combination of tastes is so fantastic that it is equally delicious hot or cold. Now that you can get hold of these beans year round, the fun of the expectation of the new season is lost. I eat them warm in winter and cold in summer. They can be used to accompany any meat or fish dish.

If you are using lemon, add it at the last minute because it will discolour the beans quickly.

METHOD

Simmer the beans in plenty of well salted boiling water until *al dente*. Drain well and transfer to a bowl. Mix with the mint, garlic, olive oil and season just to taste. Allow to cool, tossing the beans from time to time. Stir in the lemon juice or wine vinegar, if you wish, when you are about to serve the beans.

VEGETALI ARROSTITI
Chargrilled Vegetables

SERVES 4

250 g (9 oz) fennel

120 g (4½ oz) courgettes

150 g (5 oz) Jerusalem artichokes

250 g (9 oz) aubergine

75 g (3 oz) radicchio

225 g (8 oz) red pepper

120 g (4½ oz) mushrooms (shiitake, oyster or field)

FOR THE MARINADE

6 tablespoons extra virgin olive oil

½ garlic clove, crushed

1 tablespoon very finely chopped fresh flat-leaf parsley

Juice ½ lemon

Sea salt

1 garlic bulb, to garnish

The entire world seems to have been caught up by the grilled vegetable craze, from California to New York, Paris and Rome, perhaps the best example of today's trend for healthy eating. I firmly believe that there is space in this world for any kind of food and I eat this dish because I like it and not because it is fashionable. In fact, I forget all about meat when I eat it.

The process of blanching is essential for the root vegetables because if they are not blanched, they will char on the outside by the time the centre is cooked.

I like to use Radicchio di Treviso, an elongated version of the more familiar radicchio, sold with its root attached. If you can't get it, use ordinary radicchio.

METHOD

Preheat the grill or griddle.

Cut the fennel into 5 mm (¼ in) slices, vertically. Cut the courgettes and aubergine into 5 mm (¼ in) slices lengthwise. Peel the Jerusalem artichokes and cut into 5 mm (¼ in) slices. If using Radicchio di Treviso, peel the root and cut in half. Seed the pepper and cut into quarters lengthwise. Trim the mushroom stalks.

In a pan of salted boiling water, blanch the fennel and artichokes for 3 minutes, drain and refresh in plenty of very cold water. Pat dry with kitchen paper.

Mix the marinade ingredients. Using a brush, baste the sliced vegetables and place on the grill or griddle. Brown slowly on both sides. Remove and baste again. Repeat until all the vegetables are cooked. Arrange on a preheated serving dish and decorate with fried, unpeeled garlic cloves as in the picture on page 174.

POMODORI RIPIENI
Stuffed Tomatoes

SERVES 4

4 x 200 g (7 oz) large ripe beef tomatoes

75 g (3 oz) fresh white breadcrumbs

2 tablespoons chopped fresh basil

2 tablespoons chopped fresh mint

½ garlic clove, crushed

Sea salt

2 tablespoons extra virgin olive oil

One of the thousand ways of using tomatoes is as a container, enclosing some spicy ingredients. When cooked in the oven, the moisture in the tomato flesh concentrates the flavour of the stuffing. You end up with a dish which is sweet, provided you use ripe tomatoes, yet savoury.

You can find this type of dish throughout the Mediterranean, stuffed with various fillings, including rice. I love it like this as a little snack or as part of an antipasto.

METHOD

Preheat the oven to 240°C/475°F/Gas 9.

Cut the top off each tomato to form a lid and scoop out the seeds. Chop this central pulp and mix with the breadcrumbs, basil, mint, garlic and salt to taste. Refill the tomatoes and transfer to an ovenproof dish that will just hold them. Sprinkle with olive oil. Return the lids and bake in the oven for 30 minutes.

Following pages (from left): *Vegetali Arrostiti* (page 172); *Finocchio Gratinato* (page 170)

CICORIA IN UMIDO
Braised Chicory

SERVES 4

750 g (1¾ lb) Belgian chicory

4 tablespoons extra virgin olive oil

2 garlic cloves, coarsely sliced

1 tablespoon small capers, drained

2 small tomatoes, sliced

Sea salt

300 ml (½ pint) chicken stock, or a bouillon cube

We usually make this dish using an Italian chicory called puntarelle. *Belgian chicory is available everywhere and is also ideal for this recipe as it offers a certain interesting bitterness. Radicchio is another possibility.*

METHOD

Cut the chicory in half lengthwise and remove and discard the tough central core, which may be bitter. Blanch in plenty of salted boiling water for 2 minutes. Drain well and place in a flameproof casserole. Sprinkle over the olive oil, garlic, capers, tomatoes and salt. Pour over the stock, cover with a lid and braise over a gentle heat for about 30 minutes, until tender.

BIETOLE BRASATE
Braised Swiss Chard

SERVES 4

**400 g (14 oz) Swiss chard
stalks**

3 tablespoons olive oil

1 small garlic clove, chopped

½ red chilli pepper (optional)

1 glass water

Salt

This is a useful vegetable to accompany various dishes. The taste reminds me slightly of spinach because it comes from the same family. I'm told that Swiss chard contains lots of trace elements and iron is the predominant one. Another chance to imitate Popeye!

METHOD

Clean the Swiss chard stalks and cut into small strips.

Heat the oil in a frying pan, add the garlic and chilli if desired and fry gently for a minute, taking care not to burn it. Then add the Swiss chard and stir fry. Add the water. Cover with a lid and cook until tender, mixing from time to time. This should take about 20 minutes. Season and serve with *Luganiga al Vino Rosso* (see page 128) or other meat dishes.

CAVOLO CAPPUCCIO ALLO SPECK
Savoy Cabbage with Speck

SERVES 4

25 g (1 oz) lean *speck* in one piece, 3 mm (⅛ in) thick

½ garlic clove, very finely chopped

¼ fresh red chilli, chopped, or to taste

2 tablespoons extra virgin olive oil

350 g (12 oz) Savoy cabbage, finely shredded

350 ml (12 fl oz) chicken stock, or a bouillon cube

Sea salt and freshly ground black pepper

This and the dish of Cavolo Rosso con Mele *(see page 162) belong more to the German-speaking part of Italy than anywhere else. Serve with crusted polenta or to accompany roast goose.*

METHOD

Cut the *speck* into thin strips.

Fry the *speck*, garlic and chilli in the oil over a moderate heat for about 5 minutes until lightly browned. Add the cabbage and stock, salt and pepper to taste and cover with a lid. Simmer for about 30 minutes or until *al dente*.

Italians use the most wonderful array of vegetables

PATATE DEI MONACI
Monks' Potatoes

SERVES 4

750 g (1¾ lb) potatoes, peeled

1 medium-sized onion

3 sprigs rosemary

Salt and freshly ground black pepper

5 tablespoons olive oil

The monks at the monastery in Taggia enjoyed this side dish with the Coniglio San Domenico (see page 123) but you can serve it with any stewed or roast meat, as well as fish. It is very simple to prepare and delicious!

METHOD

Preheat the oven to 220°C/425°F/Gas 7.

Peel and wash the potatoes. Dry with a cloth and cut each potato in half lengthways and cut in thick slices. Roughly slice the onion. Put potatoes and onion in a roasting dish, add the rosemary, season with salt and pepper and add the olive oil. Mix well. Roast in the oven for 25–30 minutes.

PEPERONI AL BALSAMICO
Peppers in Balsamic Vinegar

SERVES 4

3 red peppers

3 yellow peppers

6 tablespoons olive oil

2 garlic cloves

2 tablespoons balsamic vinegar

Salt to taste

One of the most famous producers of traditional balsamic vinegar is Signora Giacobazzi of Modena who loves her wooden barrels so much that she treats them as if they were her best friends. A wooden barrel that holds cooked-down unfermented wine must for up to 50 years and turns it into one of the most sublime and precious condiments on earth has to be your best friend!

To savour this dish it is not necessary to use a 50-year-old balsamic vinegar – a good quality younger more commercial one is fine.

METHOD

Cut the peppers in half, discard the seeds and the stem and cut into strips. Put the olive oil in a frying pan with the peppers on a high heat. When the peppers begin to sizzle loudly, turn them from time to time with a wooden spoon and repeat this to avoid them burning on either side. When the edges begin to brown, add the garlic, which needs to be cooked for a few minutes. Still on a high heat, add the salt and balsamic vinegar. Stir to evaporate the vinegar.

This dish goes well with *Anitra alla Verdi* (see page 124) or pork dishes, or it can be eaten by itself.

FORMAG
cheese and desserts

In traditional Italian meals, cheese is served before the dessert. The cheese course is called *formaggio da tavola* and it usually consists of a soft cheese such as Stracchino or Taleggio, or, as in every Italian trattoria outside Italy, Gorgonzola or Bel Paese. You can occasionally choose between Mozzarella di Bufala or Ricotta di Pecora, or even Mascarpone. It is also now very popular to have *Grana con le Pere*, a rather young Parmigiano cheese served in flakes accompanied by fresh pears. Cheese is eaten with either *grissini* or bread, never with butter or celery.

Another new cheese to look out for is Crutin (not to be confused with the French goat's cheese, Crotin, which is very different). Crutin is a cheese made with equal quantities of cows' and sheep's milk to which are added pieces of black (usually summer) truffle and the aroma of the white Alba truffle. *Cruta*, in the Piemontese dialect, is the word for the cellar in which the cheeses are kept for ageing. It was found that cheese aged where Alba truffles were stored would absorb the truffles' aroma. Hence the creation of a new product in search of a new market. Considering how popular it is in my restaurant and our shop, it will soon be very widely enjoyed!

Italians love to finish a meal with something sweet, which is why the actual dessert comes at the very end of the meal. In truth, however, Italians are not renowned for their desserts – they often prefer to finish a meal with wonderful fresh ripe fruit in season placed in a bowl filled with ice cubes. I cannot think of anything nicer than cleansing the palate with some delicious fruit, fruit salad, wild strawberries or *frutti di bosco* (mixed berries), to which lemon juice and sugar are sometimes added to sharpen the taste. It may be

Previous pages: *Nocino* (page 195)

fish, white meat, red meat and game, which makes it possible to be more precise. Though it is not impossible to drink a chilled light red like a Bardolino or a Grignolino with a very strong savoury flavoured grilled fish like swordfish or tuna, generally for fish the rule is dry white wine. For this I would recommend a Gavi di Gavi, or the excellent Pomino il Benefizio made by my friend Frescobaldi, whose family has been making wine for 600 years. Also Bianco di Custoza, Pinot Bianco and Verdicchio, up to the heavier Greco di Tufo, which I would drink also with a mildly flavoured chicken dish.

For white meat like veal, turkey, chicken or rabbit, the rule is light red like Valpolicella, but also a Barbaresco, Franciacorta, Sassella or Grumello. Barbera Stradivario goes well with wild red meat. The highest category of reds is reserved for the very noble dishes of game and *funghi*, which Italy is particularly fond of in season. Pheasant, partridge, duck, and goose require a strong wine like an old Barbaresco or a good Rosso di Montalcino or Montepulciano d'Abruzzo. Even a glass or two of Amarone could go well with a fatty goose, while the King of Wines, Barolo, should ideally be drunk with a good dish of *camoscio* (wild goat) and polenta or venison with *porcini*. Also in this category are superior-league wines like Brunello di Montalcino, Tignanello, Sassicaia and Solaia. It is a pity that the British grouse, which I adore, has no matching counterpart in Italy, but, to satisfy your curiosity, I would drink a good Barbaresco or 1988 Gaja, whose producer is very extravagant with prices but makes very good wine!

For cheese the Italians do not have the same culinary culture as their French cousins, and so from medium-bodied to strong red wines, all are possible. Italy can boast the biggest variety of dessert wines because almost every region produces one or two *passitos* to go with the pud! Look at Piemonte, with its unique Moscato d'Asti or Moscato di Canelli, or Dogliani or the simple Asti Spumante, which is produced from the Muscat grape but not entirely fermented to achieve a high level of residual sugar and low alcohol content with an incredible aroma and bouquet. A well-chilled Moscato Naturale, produced in Piemonte, with its natural sparkle is perhaps one of the best and lightest of dessert wines. It is drunk with all sorts of puddings, but especially with a slice of *panettone* to celebrate Christmas.

Passitos are stronger wines obtained usually by picking the grape quite late, thus allowing the berries to become more sugary and alcoholic when turned into wine. Another way is to collect very ripe grapes and lay them on straw mats for further drying to obtain the same result as with the delayed harvest. All these wines have a natural sweetness and a complex bouquet, as well as a high degree of alcohol reaching 16 or 17 per cent by volume. To this category belong Malvasia from Piemonte and Passito di Caluso, Picolit, Moscato Rosa, Torcolato from Veneto, Sciacchetrà from Liguria, Vin Santo from Tuscany, Monica di Sardegna, Salice Salenico Aleatico from Puglia, the Lacrima Christi di Campania, Greco Bianco of Calabria and the various Passito di Pantelleria and Marsalas from Sicily. Most of these wines are drunk chilled, but some Marsalas – the semi-dry old ones – should not be and are best served at room temperature with almond-based biscuits or cakes such as *crostate di frutta* and *pastiera di grano*, typical of Napoli.

Whatever occasion you have to cater for, remember that Italy can now offer any kind of wine you may require – just ask your trusted supplier for more information.

INDEX

BIBLIOGRAPHY

When picking wild mushrooms,
always first consult a reference book
on the subject, such as:
A Passion for Mushrooms – Antonio
Carluccio (Pavilion, 1989)
Mushrooms – Roger Phillips (Elmtree,
1983).

fashionable to put balsamic vinegar on strawberries, but it is not a combination for me.

Italy probably has the best ice-cream makers in the world, so, not surprisingly, ice-creams and sorbets are very popular Italian desserts. Also on offer are an array of specialities such as the very famous *Tiramisù* (literally pick-me-up), an Italian version of *Zuppa Inglese* or English trifle, which is sophisticated in its simplicity. The ever-resourceful Italians also invented *Panna Cotta*, a subtle version of the French *Crème Brûlée*. A popular winter choice from the *carrello* (sweet trolley) are *Crostate di Frutta*, mostly made with home-made jam, and baked or cooked fruit such as pears, peaches or apples.

More exuberant and elaborate desserts include *Semi Freddo* (half cold), so called because it is neither ice-cream nor cream. Italians never add fluid double cream to anything, but a little dollop of *panna montata* (whipped cream), which is usually already sweetened in Italy, may land, if you request it, on your plate.

Other specialities such as *panettone* or *colomba* are baked for the celebration of Christmas and Easter, and there are many local regional variations of these recipes for cakes or tarts.

A very pleasant way to finish a meal, especially in Tuscany, is to dip some *cantucci* (little almond biscuits) or *anicini* (see page 196) in Vin Santo, the Tuscan dessert wine. Many Italians, however, drink Asti Spumante, the very famous Muscat wine from Monferrato, with dessert. There is however an infinite variety of excellent dessert wines to choose from.

PERE AL VINO BIANCO
Pears in White Wine

SERVES 4

4 x 200 g (7 oz) ripe pears, peeled

3 cloves

2.5 cm (1 in) cinnamon stick

Zest ¼ lemon, cut into julienne strips

50 g (2 oz) caster sugar

350 ml (12 fl oz) dry white wine

FOR THE CREAM

150 ml (¼ pint) whipping cream, whipped to form soft peaks

2 tablespoons Poire William liqueur

2 tablespoons caster sugar

I like this just as it is, well chilled, but should you want to make it more special, serve it with a bowl of vanilla ice-cream or with hot chocolate sauce.

METHOD

Choose a stainless steel saucepan that will hold the pears tightly upright to avoid using a lot of wine. Add the cloves, cinnamon stick, lemon zest and caster sugar and pour in the white wine to cover the pears. Cover with a lid and simmer gently for 25 minutes, turning the pears after 10 minutes.

Remove the pears from the liquor and cool. Boil and reduce the liquor by half. Gently fold the liqueur and caster sugar into the whipped cream. Serve the pears sliced but still attached to the stalk. Spoon over some of the liquor and the flavoured cream.

PESCHE UBRIACHE
Drunk Peaches

SERVES 4

500 g (1¼ lb) peaches, washed and cut into 8 small slices

40 g (1½ oz) caster sugar

1½ teaspoons ground cinnamon

400 ml (14 fl oz) dry red wine (such as Chianti or Dolcetto – the better the wine, the better the dish)

I was in Paris eating in my favourite restaurant, L'Ami Louis, *and after a delightful meal I was stunned when the waiter suggested I had a dessert which originates in Piemonte! In summer when you have super ripe peaches, turn the last glass of wine on the table into your dessert. You cut a few peach slices and soak them in the glass of wine. With a fork or spoon remove each peach slice and drink some wine with it.*

It is one of the most simple but most satisfying ends to a meal in the summer; naturally you see this done only in some family-run trattorie.

This is a rather posher version.

METHOD

Mix together the sugar, cinnamon and red wine and pour over the peach slices in a bowl. Chill well for 1 hour, then serve.

TIRAMISÙ DI ALESSANDRO
Alessandro's Pick-Me-Up

SERVES 4

2 eggs

2 tablespoons caster sugar

Few drops of vanilla essence

250 g (9 oz) Mascarpone

Milk, if necessary

20 Savoiardi biscuits

180 ml (6 fl oz) strong black espresso coffee

4 tablespoons Marsala

½ tablespoon cocoa powder

I was brought up in a family where good food is very important – the preparation as well as the eating. So when I was in Italy recently I was glad to see that one of my nephews, Alessandro, has inherited the family's culinary enthusiasm. I watched him making tiramisù, *a popular dessert with various versions in Italy. This is one of the simplest, but the most traditional.*

Because this recipe includes raw egg, it should be consumed immediately.

METHOD

Separate the eggs and beat the yolks with the sugar and vanilla essence. Add the Mascarpone and mix well to a creamy consistency, adding a little milk if the mixture is too thick. In another bowl beat the egg whites until stiff, then fold them into the Mascarpone mixture.

Mix the coffee and Marsala in a bowl and dip in each biscuit for a second or two, making sure they do not break. Line the bases of four bowls with the biscuits, top with the Mascarpone mixture and chill for an hour. Dust with cocoa powder and serve.

PERE AL VIN SANTO
Pears in Vin Santo

SERVES 4

4 Comice pears

1 x 750 ml bottle Vin Santo

100 g (4 oz) caster sugar

Rind of 1 lemon

3 cloves

1 stick of cinnamon

As a rule, in Italy dessert means fresh fruit. During the summer you are likely to get a basket of whatever is in season: cherries in June, apricots and plums in July, peaches and pears in August and then grapes. But in winter, baked or poached fruit like pears is very welcome.

I find that the standard compote of apples mixed with other fruit can be boring, so here I have poached pears in Vin Santo and spices to create something truly wonderful.

METHOD

First, peel the pears so that they can absorb the taste and golden colour of the wine, but leave them whole. Put them in a stainless steel saucepan just large enough to hold them and cover with the wine. Add the sugar, lemon rind and spices and poach for 40 minutes with the lid on. Remove the lid and cook for a further 10 minutes. Remove the pears from the liquid and set on one side. Boil the remaining liquid fast to reduce it to a thicker consistency. Pour this sauce over the pears, allow to cool and chill.

Following pages (from left): *Tiramisù di Allesandro* (page 188); *Pere al Vin Santo* (above); *Pesche di Giulietta* (page 194)

CROSTATA DI MELECOTOGNE
Quince Tart

MAKES 1 x 23 cm (9 in) TART

FOR THE PASTRY

4 tablespoons olive oil (not virgin)

4 tablespoons white wine, preferably sweet

40 g (1½ oz) caster sugar

150 g (5 oz) plain white flour

FOR THE FILLING

800 g (1 lb 10 oz) quince, pealed, cored and chopped into small chunks

Juice 1 lemon

3 cloves

1 cinnamon stick

300 ml (10 fl oz) water

400 g (14 oz) sugar

Quince is the fruit that most reminds me of my grandmother, who used to preserve them in various ways so that they could be enjoyed during the winter months. Still today, this fruit remains one of my favourites for making jams and compotes.

Here I have added lemon juice so the fruit does not discolour as well as a lot of sugar to compensate for its acidity. To counterbalance the calories, the pastry of this crostata *is made with olive oil instead of butter and eggs which is a good substitute for anyone who cannot eat dairy products.*

METHOD

Preheat the oven to 240°C, 475°F, Gas 9.

To make the pastry, put the oil, wine and sugar in a bowl and mix thoroughly. Fold in the flour to form a dough. Knead with your hands until smooth. Wrap the pastry in cling film and place in the fridge for about 20 minutes. On a floured surface, roll out with a rolling pin to a thickness of 3 mm (⅛ in). Line a greased 23 cm (9 in) flan tin with the pastry and bake blind for 10–12 minutes.

To make the filling, put the chunks of quince in a pan with the lemon juice, cloves, cinnamon and water. Cook until the fruit begins to soften and dissolve. Add the sugar and continue to cook for about 35–40 minutes or until it begins to resemble jam. (Please note that if you wish to use this as jam and preserve it for a long

FOR THE TOPPING

600 g (1 lb 6 oz) quince, peeled, quartered and cored

400 g (14 oz) sugar

Juice 1 lemon

Water, enough to cover the fruit

Icing sugar, for dredging

time, you must use 700 g (1 lb 6 oz) of sugar to 1 kg (2¼ lb) of fruit.) Leave this mixture to cool. Remove the cinnamon stick.

Meanwhile to make the topping, put the quartered and cored pieces of quince in a pan with the sugar and lemon juice and cover with water. Place on the heat and simmer for 30 minutes.

Fill the pastry case with the cooled filling mixture and spread evenly with a palette knife. Then remove the poached quince pieces from the water and slice thinly and evenly. Arrange these slices on top of the tart decoratively. Dredge with icing sugar and place under a hot grill for a couple of minutes or until the sugar begins to bubble. This will give a nice glaze.

Serve with cream, if desired.

PESCHE
DI GIULIETTA
Juliette's Peaches

SERVES 4

4 large, ripe peaches

4 or 5 cloves

Half a cinnamon stick

Rind 1 lime

**1 litre (1¾ pints) Soave white
wine**

300 g (11 oz) caster sugar

4 tablespoons Amaretto

Soft Amaretti biscuits, to serve

Don't imagine that because this recipe includes sugar that you can get away with using unripe peaches – you always get out of a dish what you put in. What you need here are large, juicy, tree-ripened peaches, such as those grown around Verona, which are ideal for this wonderful dessert.

I created this recipe to celebrate Juliette's birthday in Verona.

METHOD

Wash the peaches and put in a pan just large enough to hold them. Add the spices, the lime rind and the wine (which should cover the peaches) and poach for 20 minutes. Remove the peaches from the cooking liquid, taking care not to damage the skin. Add the sugar to the wine and reduce until you get a syrupy consistency. Remove from the heat, allow to cool then add the Amaretto and chill.

To serve, place the peaches in individual dishes, pour the sauce over them and serve with Amaretti biscuits. Cream and whipped cream aren't very Italian, so I leave that up to you!

NOCINO
Walnut Liqueur

8 green walnuts, quartered

1 litre (2 pints) vodka or
   schnapps

1 cinnamon stick

20 cloves

1 teaspoon grated nutmeg

300 g (11 oz) caster sugar

June 24, the feast of St John, is a very important date for those making Nocino. *It is a very simple liqueur drunk not only in Emilia Romagna where everyone makes it, but all over Italy. In Modena there is a club which takes* Nocino-*making and tasting very seriously . . . until, that is, the members have had a few glasses!*

There are people who say that witches dance around the walnut tree on the night of June 23–24, but in fact the reason why this date is important is that, at this time of year the walnuts are still soft inside and easy to cut, just right for making Nocino.

The second main ingredient of this liqueur is pure alcohol, which you can buy freely in Italy, although it is subject to a special Government tax. This 95 per cent alcohol (by volume) is highly inflammable, and is later diluted with water and brought to the usual drinkable strength. In countries where it is not possible to buy such alcohol, you can use strong vodka or schnapps to make Nocino.

METHOD

Place all the ingredients, except the sugar, in a glass jar and leave to marinate in a sunny place for 40 days. During this time, the liquid takes on a dark colour. Dissolve the sugar in the soaking liquid, and strain everything thoroughly, discarding the walnuts and spices.

Keep the liqueur in small bottles and serve very small amounts after special meals!

ANICINI DI ORVIETO
Orvieto Aniseed Biscuits

MAKES APPROXIMATELY 20 BISCUITS

100 ml (3½ fl oz) olive oil

100 ml (3½ fl oz) white wine, preferably sweet

75 g (3 oz) caster sugar

150 g (5 oz) plain white flour

½ teaspoon bicarbonate of soda

2 teaspoons anise

1 teaspoon fennel seeds

I wanted to recreate this recipe after having seen and tasted these biscuits in a very fine delicatessen in Orvieto. They are good dipped in a dessert wine, as they do locally, or simply eaten as a biscuit. Since they are made with olive oil instead of butter, they are suitable for people who cannot eat dairy products.

METHOD

Preheat the oven to 150°C, 300°F, Gas Mark 2. Line a baking tray with greaseproof paper.

Put the oil, wine and sugar in a bowl and mix thoroughly. Then fold in the flour, bicarbonate of soda and spices.

Place teaspoons of the mixture onto the baking tray, spacing them well apart as they will spread during baking. Place in the oven and bake for 13 minutes or until golden brown.

Leave to cool on a wire rack so they become hard.

LA DELIZIA DEI DOGI
Doges' Delight Ice-Cream

MAKES 6 SERVINGS OF EACH FLAVOUR

FOR THE CINNAMON

500 ml (17 fl oz) full-fat milk

150 ml (¼ pint) double cream

2 tablespoons ground cinnamon

2 cloves

6 egg yolks

50 g (2 oz) honey (optional)

150 g (5 oz) caster sugar

FOR THE CARDAMOM

500 ml (17 fl oz) full-fat milk

1 tablespoon cardamom seeds, crushed

6 egg yolks

50 g (2 oz) honey (optional)

150 g (5 oz) sugar

4 oz pistachio nuts

150 ml (¼ pint) double cream

Green food colouring

FOR THE SAFFRON

500 ml (17 fl oz) full-fat milk

Pinch of saffron

6 egg yolks

50 g (2 oz) honey (optional)

100 g (4 oz) sugar

150 ml (¼ pint) double cream

I invented this recipe during a New Year's holiday in Venice in honour of the Doges, who were very much involved in bringing back from their expeditions in the Mediterranean all sorts of spices previously unknown in Italy. It uses saffron, the most precious of all spices, cardamom and cinnamon to make three ice-creams whose flavours blend marvellously well together.

METHOD

The method is similar, for each ice-cream flavour. In separate saucepans, bring to the boil the milk, cinnamon and cloves, milk and cardamom seeds, and milk and saffron. Simmer for 5–10 minutes. Allow to cool and strain.

In separate bowls mix the eggs, honey (if using) and the required quantity of sugar until creamy. To each bowl add the flavoured milk a little at a time and whisk until it is all used up. Place the mixture back in the appropriate pans and cook in a bain-marie (a bowl over simmering hot water) for 15 minutes or until the mixture coats the back of a spoon. In order to avoid lumps, keep stirring. Leave for one or two days in the fridge. If you don't or can't, the texture and flavour of the finished result will not be as good, but you can cheat and put in a blender.

Then churn (in an ice-cream machine) for about 30 minutes. Add the semi-whipped cream (plus peeled, chopped pistachios and green colouring for the cardamom flavour) in the last 5 minutes, continue to churn and freeze.

Serve all three flavours together.

ITALIAN WINES

I will only be able to give a brief description of Italian wines and what they are to be drunk with – it would take a whole book to mention them all and do a proper analysis. For far too long, Italian wines have suffered a mixed reputation in the international market. Although Italy was one of the first nations in the world to produce this delectable fermented grape juice and became quantitatively the biggest wine producer in the world, it was necessary not only to have good marketing to confirm the excellence of already established wines, but also to raise general levels of quality and value for money. The old name for Italy was Enotria, from the Greek word for wine, *oinos*: the 'land of wine'. The spread of Italian restaurants all over the world confirmed that reputation.

Now the situation has changed drastically, dictated by tougher competition from countries such as Australia, New Zealand, South Africa and the USA that have recently discovered their viticultural potential. Far-sighted Italian producers like the Tuscan Marchese Piero Antinori (just to mention the most famous) started to look many years ago at how the French, with no better soil or geographic location than Italy's, nor the wide variety of grapes available to the Italians, were able to produce so many recognized wines of such outstanding quality. Antinori discovered first how to treat the vine, and then made improvements all along the line to the marketing of the wine. He borrowed one or two wonderful wine technicians and there we are!

Many others followed the Marchese in improving variety and making better wine. Italy can now be proud to offer a very wide selection of wines, from almost every region, which are able to compete at the highest level. Having been a wine merchant myself for a long time, and now as a restaurateur at the receiving end, I notice this particularly, being constantly confronted with good offers of price in relation to quality. Slowly but surely, customers are asking for particular Italian wines, until now unknown, which they consume with great pleasure. Incidentally, generally speaking, I really believe the British are excellent wine connoisseurs – in some cases even better than the Italians and the French. Although Britain was always a wine producer in Roman times, only now are attempts being made to produce something drinkable. Traditionally therefore interest has been directed towards wine from other countries, especially those where British people travelled extensively. It is sufficient to look at some of the wine auctions of deceased generals or barristers to know what treasures they were keeping in their cellars.

Following modern trends and enthusiasms, the Italians, or the worst of their producers, thought they could make big money using two specific elements, the Chardonnay grape and the barrique. It is now clear that Chardonnay has been misused worldwide because it is so easy to grow and adaptable to most climates and soils; and similarly with barriques, the small oak barrels capable of imparting wines kept in them for a short time with the oaky taste that characterizes the most prestigious French produce. Whenever I can I encourage Italian wine producers not to think so simply, but to experiment with other varieties which, if treated well, will give better results.

I have never been a snob about wines – what counts is how your personal palate appreciates it. To this end I could say that wine is good when you like it although there are certainly some guidelines that can help us to a better understanding of the drink.

I appreciate a glass or two whilst eating food. Wine should never be used simply as a vehicle for forgetting one's troubles or losing one's inhibitions, but should be a respected part of the meal, one that is able either to reinforce or annihilate the taste of the food. That's why it is so important to choose the right wine.

I quite like, for example, the habit in the Veneto of decanting Prosecco irreverently into a glass jug. This has the simple effect of removing the eventually superfluous sparkle. Done in Venice, this is fine. Done in London or elsewhere and perhaps with Champagne, it would look like pretentious understatement. A friend of mine, Giovanni Gregoletto, a wine producer from Valdobbiadene, near Conegliano, where most Prosecco is produced, has called his own wine 'Ombra' (shade), because the place where people enjoy this little treat is in the Piazza San Marco, in the shade of the *campanile*, the famous bell tower. So in Venice, when you want to drink a small glass of Prosecco, you just say '*un ombra per favore*'. Or if a Venetian wants to invite a friend for a chat and a drink: '*Vieni andiamo a prenderci un ombretta*' – come, we're going to have an *ombretta*, which is a cosy name for *ombra*. This nice habit unfortunately does not know when to stop!

Other producer-friends of mine, the Famiglia Bava in Cocconato, in the province of Asti, combine the sounds of popular local instruments with their wines. In fact, Roberto Bava believes that the character of a specific wine has an affinity with the type of sound a specific instrument is capable of making. And so he invites lots of friends to drinking concert sessions to verify that what he says is true. At the beginning of a concert tasting, perhaps you are not totally convinced; but, certainly, after tasting Barbera Stradivario and Bombardina Dolcetto and Moscato Trombone accompanied by sublime music played by the students of the Accademia Musicale di Torino, you will change your mind!

The idea behind combining wine and food is that they should complement each other. There shouldn't be too big a contrast. Certainly, as an aperitif you can drink a dry sparkling wine, usually one from the Veneto, like Prosecco, but also heavier southern wines like dry Sicilian Marsala (which equals a good sherry) or an Erbaluce di Piemonte, or even a Blanc de Morgex, a delightful sparkling white wine from the Aosta valley (where they speak French).

We come then to *antipasti*, which are a little difficult to accompany because of the many pickled items made purposely to whet the appetite. We know that vinegar or the acid in lemon and suchlike can kill the best of wines. Usually a dry white is suggested, like a Soave or a Pinot Grigio from Veneto or Orvieto Secco from Umbria, but you can also try a Pigato from Liguria or the new Galestro from Tuscany. It is also possible to take a chilled dry Lambrusco with all the hams and salamis from Emilia-Romagna, but perhaps better to stay with the white Trebbiano from the same area.

First courses are also not easy to accompany due to the extreme variety of tastes. It is impossible to state what to drink with pasta or with risotto or polenta. The basic rule is to drink the local wine, and there are many, observing the rule that the spicier the food the stronger or even more colourful the wine. Dolcetto from Piemonte, for example, goes very well with *agnolotti*, a sort of Piemontese meat ravioli; while a good risotto with truffles should be accompanied by a gentle Barbaresco. Other wines for the first course are a young Chianti (not a *riserva*, which is older) or a Gewürztraminer from Tyrol. To be washed down properly, a lasagne requires a good Sangiovese, while polenta with ragù of chicken or rabbit should be combined with Carema, a strong Nebbiolo made by my old schoolfriend, Luigi Ferrando.

Main courses are easier to combine because of the clear division between

Following pages: A selection of Italian wines and cheese with (foreground left) *Crostata di Melecotogne* (page 192) and (centre) *Anicini di Orvieto* (page 196)